Dream Job Profiles

LOOK FOR THESE OTHER GRAPHIA BOOKS

Whatcha Mean, What's a Zine?
The Art of Making Zines and Mini-Comics
by Mark Todd and Esther Pearl Watson

Dunk
by David Lubar

Open the Unusual Door: True Life Stories of Challenge, Adventure, and Success by Black Americans
edited by Barbara Summers

Real Time
by Pnina Moed Kass

What Your Mama Never Told You: True Stories About Sex and Love
edited by Tara Roberts

Zen and the Art of the SAT:
How to Think, Focus, and Achieve Your Highest Score
by Matt Bardin and Susan Fine

After Summer
by Nick Earls

I Just Hope It's Lethal: Poems of Sadness, Madness, and Joy
edited by Liz Rosenberg and Deena November

Kid B
by Linden Dalecki

Dream Job PROFILES

THE YOUNG & SUCCESSFUL SHARE THEIR SECRETS

DONNA HAYDEN GREEN

GRAPHIA

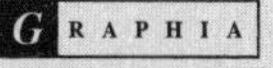

AN IMPRINT OF HOUGHTON MIFFLIN COMPANY BOSTON 2006

 Published in the United States by Graphia, an imprint of Houghton Mifflin Company, Boston, Massachusetts.

For information about permission to reproduce selections from this book, write to Permissions, Houghton Mifflin Company, 215 Park Avenue South, New York, New York 10003.

www.houghtonmifflinbooks.com

Graphia and the Graphia logo are registered trademarks of Houghton Mifflin Company.

The text of this book is set in 10-point Palatino.

Library of Congress Cataloging-in-Publication Data
Green, Donna, 1956–
Dream job profiles : the young and successful share their secrets / by Donna Hayden Green.
p. cm.
ISBN-13: 978-0-618-56320-3 (pbk. : alk. paper)
ISBN-10: 0-618-56320-2 (pbk. : alk. paper)
1. Occupations. 2. Vocational guidance. 3. Professions. 4. Vocational interests—United States—Case studies. 5. Successful people—Case studies. I. Title.
HF5382.G73 2006
650.1—dc22
2006004462

Manufactured in the United States of America
HAD 10 9 8 7 6 5 4 3 2 1

To James Daw, business columnist with the Toronto Star, *for making his job one of the most important in the world.*

CONTENTS

What work I have done I have done because it has been play. If it had been work I shouldn't have done it.

—Mark Twain

Introduction

These are the stories of people who took some age-old wisdom and flung it to the floor. The people you will soon meet turned their back on security and followed their passion with abandon—well, in truth, with calculated focus and drive—and transformed their fascination into something gratifying *and* money-making. No stuffy accounting practice by day, garage grunge band by night here.

All these intrepid under-thirties have jobs most people would die for—the general manager of a professional sports team, the manager of one of the hottest indie bands in the United States, a biologist who rescues manatees, a celebrity interviewer, a web-comic duo, an assistance dog trainer, an outdoor educator, a scientist who explores Mars, a makeup artist, and even the mayor of a postcard-perfect small town.

There's no law that says what they've done can't be repeated in the area of your passion. In fact, the odds may be stacked in favor of any teen who tries. Many of the people here started by doing volunteer work or minimum-wage grunt jobs until, by sheer determination, they were there when the chance came to do something more meaningful.

I hope this book ignites your ambition to go for the job that thrills you, and gives you some know-how to make it happen.

Dream Job Profiles

The Power of Just Asking

FREDDY MEDILL

CELEBRITY HOLLYWOOD REPORTER

Freddy Medill was chatting up Hollywood's most beautiful actresses when most of his classmates were still trying to overcome their fear of looking stupid in front of the opposite sex. Freddy's gorgeous interview subjects gush over his blond head. They bend forward, smiling invitingly. They almost press his forehead to their breasts. Standing close enough to hear her breathe, he tells Cameron Diaz he has a way with women. She throws her head back laughing, but we know it's true. Freddy has a way with everyone, it seems, even when he was fourteen.

Skeptical? Check out Freddy's interview with Diaz on his website, www.fredtv.net. You'll see there that Diaz is hardly the only celebrity he has charmed. Freddy is the creator, producer, and star of *Fred TV*, a show featuring interviews with celebrities in entertainment, sports, and the arts.

Freddy's amazing career began with a novel idea for his bar mitzvah video when he was twelve. Instead of displaying the usual baby pictures, which he says "was basically a yawn for everybody except the parents," Freddy decided to take advantage of living in the entertainment capital of the world. He set out to shoot some celebrity interviews.

The bar mitzvah video included Larry King, Neil Sedaka, and George Foreman, among others. "These were people we just saw," says Freddy. "It was a fluke, really."

How He Asked

As it happens, Larry King dines at a Beverly Hills deli that Freddy's family frequents. One morning when Freddy was at the deli with his family, he plucked up his courage and approached King. "I asked him if we could do a little shtick and he said, 'Sure, why don't you come by the studio?' He gave me the address and the hours.

"This was before 9-11. My dad and I just walked in, put our names down. Larry King was very cool about it. After he interviewed his guest, who was U.S. press secretary Dee Dee Myers, I got to sit at the famous desk in the guest seat. I had worn my suspenders to our meeting and I said to him, 'Let's do lunch.'"

Freddy met Neil Sedaka while both the singer and the Medill family were vacationing in Hawaii. Freddy approached Sedaka in the pool area of the hotel. "I asked if I could do a little shtick with *him*. He was really cool about it. He sang 'Happy Birthday Sweet Sixteen' but with the words 'Happy Bar Mitzvah Freddy Medill' instead. That made another great piece.

"George Foreman was at a party my dad was invited to, so I went along with the camera and did a little thing with him." Freddy and his dad also caught Jay Leno in his studio after one of his shows and got him bantering with Freddy.

A professional editor whom Freddy's parents hired put the clips together, and on March 20, 1999, in front of 250 bar mitzvah guests, Freddy Medill became a celebrity interviewer.

Building on His Breaks

Two months later Freddy and his dad went to a high school silent auction that featured a pair of tickets to the premiere of Adam Sandler's movie *Big Daddy*. "If you live here," says the down-to-earth interviewer, "you get all those kinds of things popping up at silent auctions—like walk-on roles for TV shows." Freddy asked his dad to try for the tickets. "My immediate thought was that I would try to get on the press line," Freddy says. "I didn't really care about seeing the movie or going to the after-party, which was what the package was giving you." Freddy and his dad went home with the tickets.

With Freddy's goal in mind, he and his dad talked up Freddy's previous celebrity interviewing experience to the studio's publicist. It worked. On the night of the premiere, Freddy was allowed onto the press line without actual press credentials—with his dad standing by him as cameraman. Thirteen-year-old Freddy, dressed in a suit and tie, stood out in the crush of reporters, and Adam Sandler had the good grace to answer Freddy's questions.

"I was psyched, because as a younger kid, to my eyes then, he was probably the biggest star I'd talked to, and I didn't think that would happen," says Freddy. "I'm all smiles on the tape."

That summer Freddy didn't go to camp like he usually did. Instead he wrote questions, went to premieres, and started dreaming big. "In June and early July," he says, "it was a fun hobby. As the summer went on, mid-July and August, I decided I was going to work a little harder and pretended that my interviews were actually going to be on TV. I was thinking of selling my interviews that soon.

"I wore a suit to all the first events I went to. The publicists thought it was cute and people began to know me." During one of these premieres, Freddy was approached by a reporter from the *Los Angeles Times.* The reporter was curious about this unusual young man. They exchanged business cards, and a short time later she called to arrange an interview.

Freddy tells the story like this: "In December 2000, the *Los Angeles Times* wrote a story about me on the front page of the Living section. When I got home from school that day I had about 200 e-mails, from *20/20, The Tonight Show with Jay Leno, The Today Show,* and fans. That started the whole press monster. I did an interview with a radio station in San Francisco; an ABC local station did a piece on me; then I was on the *Today Show* and *Leno.*" He had just turned fifteen for the *Leno* appearance.

After seeing Freddy on *Leno,* a representative from Starz Entertainment Group, a large satellite TV provider, arranged for his celebrity interviews and premiere coverage to be aired on the Starz kids' channel, WAM!

"I've been doing premieres with them a couple of times a month ever since," says Freddy. "That was the first real paying job that came out of this. I've done four half-hour specials with them as well." Three of those specials were shot on the lot of Columbia Pictures, and one was done at Disney Studios.

For a kid in high school, the workload was impressive. "I started going to events literally every night and juggled that with school." The pressure mounted. In the second half of tenth grade, Freddy left his private Jewish school to do independent study at home with the assistance of math and English tutors.

Though he knew the media hype would be short-lived, it launched other opportunities for the indomitable Freddy apart from the talk show circuit. He was invited to be an extra in the 2002 teen movie *The New Guy,* in which he had to faint onto a mat from being in the presence of Tommy Lee.

Freddy's work is now shown regularly on the Disney Channel in the United Kingdom. As their freelance Hollywood correspondent, Freddy has access to many special opportunities, not the least of which was interviewing the stars of *The Incredibles* and meeting the animators at work in their studio. That plum gig came about through a chance meeting.

"I was doing a premiere when I was approached by an Orthodox Jew, black hat and all, who told me he worked for a TV station in England," explains Freddy. "Several months went by before I heard from him again. He changed jobs many times and made attempts to get me work in the UK and other areas 'across the pond.' He referred me to many people who contacted me with offers to do one-time junkets and other events here in Hollywood for them. Finally, through this man, came the Disney contact." And with characteristic modesty he says, "I owe him a great deal. He was very helpful to my career."

Eyes on the Stars, Feet on the Ground

Freddy's two younger brothers are anything but starstruck. "They have absolutely no interest in this," says Freddy, without a trace of disappointment. His brothers are sports fans, not movie aficionados.

Part of Freddy's charm is his disarming honesty. He knows at the beginning he got by as a novelty. He knows having two parents who are litigation lawyers living in Beverly Hills has been a big help, too. Not everyone is wealthy enough to travel in celebrity circles, and even fewer have lawyers at home to take care of their business contracts. "My father played a big part in helping me get to where I am now," acknowledges Freddy.

Freddy's father acts as his agent and manager. For a while he continued to be Freddy's cameraman at the premieres. "That was part of the unique look when we went out there," Freddy explains. "Now we have professional cameramen and soundmen, but a lot of times I still go with my dad." Some fathers and sons go to football games; Freddy and his dad go to premieres.

Freddy easily admits that having his father at the premieres with him has helped him feel supported and protected. "I know a lot of the business is crazy," he says. "There are people walking around with tattoos and purple hair and leather pants. I try to interview some of them because it's fun stuff and it really shows the atmosphere of the premieres, but I don't let the craziness influence me."

He also understands how actors' publicists and studio publicists work at odds with each other. "The studio publicists want the stars talking [to the press], but the personal publicist is more interested in making his client bigger than in making the movie bigger. It's about looking important," explains Freddy. "The first guest on *Leno*, if he or she is a big star, won't stay for the rest of the show. They want to make it look like they have better things to do."

That desire to appear in demand fuels some typical celebrity behavior at premieres. "Stars coming down the line with their cell phones, they're really talking to nobody," says Freddy. "They wear their sunglasses indoors. Publicists don't want their star to talk to every single person in that press line. Stars have to go in and see their movie even though they've seen it a million times before." Stars act this way, Freddy says, "until their stock goes down."

Freddy is aware that in this business anyone's stock can go down, including his own. "I have to understand that gigs will come and go. I was doing well because I looked young and my voice was high. I have to think about opening up doors for myself that will be long term. I'm still trying to figure out ways to expand *Fred TV*. It's fun and I want to keep this going."

Getting to the Next Step

Freddy is certainly not shy about mining the relationships he's developed with agents, publicists, managers, stars, and directors, whose names and numbers he keeps meticulously organized on his computer. "One of the most important things I've learned is to ask. You can't be afraid of a no, especially in this business. If you ask and you get rejected, it's only a no, but you are leaving the door open."

There's a never-say-die attitude in Freddy's determination, but it's rooted in practicality. "Get your face out there and ask even if you think you have no chance, even if you think Larry King is going to look at you and say, 'Are you crazy? I'm busy.' You still have to go out there and ask, because that's how people get jobs in this business."

On the red carpet during the premiere of *Wild Wild West*, in 1999, Will Smith gave Freddy a piece of advice that Smith's father had given to him: "Never let your success go to your head, and never let your failures go to your heart." Speaking of that advice Freddy says, "Once you are successful you don't want it going to your head, and on your way to getting successful you are going to go through some failures and you can't let them go to your heart, because if you do you're never going to reach the top."

Asked if he's had any failures, Freddy quickly says yes. They clearly weigh heavily on him, but as failures go, they're pretty minor. "There were times when I had the chance to interview somebody that I wouldn't get often and I would ask them a wrong question or say something that ended up offending them." He recalls one particularly embarrassing moment when he mistook one celebrity for another. Freddy asked Jamie Foxx to do a spontaneous promo for *Fred TV* and instructed him to say, "This is Damon Wayans and you're watching *Fred TV*." Foxx good-naturedly responded, "I'm not Damon Wayans but I'll do it!"

To avoid these kinds of mistakes and to make the most of the opportunities that present themselves, Freddy is conscientious about doing his research before squeezing his way to the edge of the red carpet. "You have to keep up-to-date and be prepared. You have to have a set of questions to ask even if you're not sure you're going to have a chance to talk. The interview might be over in five minutes, but the tapes last forever.

"I have over fifteen hundred tapes. If nothing else, if this just ends right now or if I never get that prime time spot on NBC or whatever, I would have some hell of a home video collection for my kids to watch."

Apart from Freddy's skill at editing and encoding the videos for his dazzling website and hosting that site, too, his excellent adventure could easily morph into a career in directing, editing, hosting TV shows, or working as a publicist or agent. That decision is still a long way away. Freddy hopes to enter UCLA and to study liberal arts, journalism, or film, but first he wants to finish a few courses at junior college which he feels he needs to overcome some shortfalls from his days of independent study at home.

In the meantime he's busy trying to get a media pass from the Academy Awards publicity team so he can cover the Oscars for Starz Encore and Disney UK. It's his third try. Every year since he was fifteen, the Oscar folks have refused to issue him press credentials that would allow him to line up with the older journalists.

Freddy feels the sting of what he considers age discrimination, but he hopes that his eighteenth birthday, combined with his ongoing relationships with Disney and Starz, will make a difference this year. "Other journalists tell me the Oscars aren't fun at all. You have to stand sideways with no room to breathe. It's hot outside. At the same time, it's the number one event in Hollywood."

He'll keep asking.

FREELANCE FREEDOM

Forget about Freddy's fabulous celebrity and glamorous gigs: he's simply a freelance reporter. A freelancer is self-employed and sells his or her work to other companies. Just about any job in media can be freelance. In fact, many of the articles you read in newspapers, magazines, and on the Internet are written by freelancer contributors. Writers, photographers, reporters, videographers, producers, editors, and directors can all be freelance. Freddy advises young freelancers to watch respected interviewers to see how they do it, and to research their backgrounds to learn how they got where they are.

The good news is that it's easy to get started as a freelancer; the challenge is getting good enough and in demand enough to make a living at it. You don't have to have something unique like a thirteen-year-old stature and good looks either. Mostly, you just need drive. Choose a subject area that interests you and a medium in which you have some rudimentary skill, and then start thinking up projects. You'll be surprised how willing most people are to help you get started.

(This author got her start, at the age of forty, by riding her bike to local businesses and interviewing the owners. Her town paper published the articles, and bigger markets followed. No dazzling charisma, no prestigious journalism training, no deep pockets of influence—just an idea and the desire to do it.)

TAKING THE PLUNGE

The first sale is the toughest, so start small. Your school newspaper or yearbook can make a great first market for budding writers and photographers: neither one will pay, but both will give you valuable experience and byline exposure. If you're a videographer, try getting something shown at a school assembly, then build to local media outlets with small audiences. You can find submission guidelines on media companies' websites or you can call to request a copy. Read the guidelines carefully. They will explain what a submission should contain, the requirements for its presentation, the pay range, where to send your submission, and the specific person it should be sent to. The most common error freelancers make is submitting something that is unlike anything the outlet publishes.

Ask yourself, would your local paper carry a story like the one you plan to send? Does your submission sound like something that could be on your favorite radio station? Do the story and visuals look like what's on the local cable channel?

Once your creation is polished, send it off—ideally to the appropriate editor's attention. Enclose a cover letter in which you introduce yourself and say you will follow up in a few weeks if you don't receive a reply sooner. Make things easy. Your submission should be easy to read or view, and your contact information, including your phone number and e-mail address, should be prominent. Attach a stamped, self-addressed envelope if you want your material returned (although some companies may have a no-return policy; check the website of each company you make a submission to for a statement on their return policy). Then do as you say and follow up, several times if necessary.

CRITICISM & REJECTION— YOUR BEST FRIENDS

Then brace yourself for rejection. Rejections can give insight into why your work may not be suitable. As Freddy says, "It's only a no." Don't be afraid to ask an editor how you can improve your work or make it more suitable for that market. Rather than asking why your work was rejected, ask—and really want to find out—how your work could have been better. Editors are notoriously busy, but some may be willing to spend a few minutes on the phone or through an e-mail explaining how a piece could be made stronger if they've had time to read your submission and if they see some promise in it. That feedback will likely be among the most valuable you will ever get. And, of course, keep trying, even with the same outlets. Persistence pays. What you lack in experience you can make up with a youthful voice, vision, and approach. Don't overlook personal essays, industry stories for trade publications, and concept videos: what seems commonplace to you may open up a new worldview to someone else.

MONEY & FAME?

In many cases pay rates are negotiable, but seldom for beginners. To learn more about general business practices, pay, and contracts, seek out the freelancers' association in your field. Do an Internet search by typing the keywords "Freelance" + [your medium]. These associations frequently have resources to help beginners.

The National Writers Union site (www.nwu.org) is directed to professional writers and their business concerns. Much of the information is restricted to members only, but the site has helpful links and affords a glimpse into the world of copyright issues. The American Society of Journalists and Authors also provides useful information for freelance writers (www.asja.org).

If you feel you've got the stuff, put yourself out there and go for it. Everyone has to start somewhere, and editors know that. You will never forget your first byline.

Using What Makes You Different

SABRINA RINALDI

MAKEUP & HAIR ARTIST

Sabrina Rinaldi was impossible not to notice in high school: outrageous hair, wild makeup, a different costume every day. While many students are happy in the morning to find pants that fit or a reasonably unwrinkled T-shirt to wear to school, Sabrina accessorized elaborately themed costumes—cheerleader, geisha, PJs, checkered old-man polyester pants, a baby blue ruffled tuxedo shirt and suspenders. The days she dressed as a waitress were her favorites. "I took a notepad to school to take people's orders in the cafeteria. My dad did my hair in a beehive with super-sixties makeup," she says, smiling.

Her *dad?*

Yes, Sabrina came by her interest in appearances honestly. Her father owned a hair salon, and her aunt operated an aesthetics studio in the basement of the salon. Now, at twenty-seven, Sabrina is the conventional-looking one, earning money making *other* people look different. Self-confident, striking, and hardly outrageous, Sabrina works as a freelance makeup and hair artist in Toronto, Canada. She does makeup and hair for rock stars, actors, models, authors, and just about anyone else whose image is going to show up in print or in a video.

The drive to look different in high school was partly artistic expression and a good part hypocrisy detector. "I wanted people to accept me for me, no matter what I looked like," Sabrina says, even if it meant her mom didn't want to be seen in a mall with her. Heavier then and pre–nose job, she says she was the subject of some mockery. "I wasn't the most attractive girl in high school. It was easier to hide behind outfits. In retrospect, it was easier on my ego for boys to reject me because I was dressed so weird."

These days her work appears in major magazines, TV commercials, and music videos, on book covers, and in newspapers, brochures, and catalogues. Catch the ad for Xbox Zoo Tycoon 2? Sabrina made the model look like a sweaty zookeeper who had been shoveling elephant dung all day. She's worked on ads for Nike, Wal-Mart, and Sears, and has even done the makeup for models on Harlequin book covers. As you might expect, she works with glamorous runway models, but she also works on servers at parties who are done up in costume, like the galas Cirque du Soleil hosts at the opening of a new show.

It's a People Business

Surprisingly, Sabrina's most enjoyable clients have been celebrated authors. "The most interesting people I've worked on were Ann-Marie MacDonald, Yann Martel, and Douglas Coupland. I did a Random House campaign. Their conversation was so interesting." She's far less fond of many of "the big names" she's encountered. "I've done some big punk rock bands, but they didn't talk to me much. People get excited hearing you work with these big bands, and yet when I work with them, I don't get a sense of who they are as people. There's a distance there."

Sabrina thrives on the personal connection she's usually good at establishing with her more ordinary, noncelebrity clients. "I'm the first person they see before they go on the set," she explains. "I warm them up, make them feel comfortable, because as soon as you're comfortable in your own skin, when you get in front of that camera you can really give to the camera; something in your eyes communicates with the audience."

It's a people business, certainly, but it's also one with a great deal of variety. "My favorite part of my job is meeting new people every day and constantly having new challenges put in front of me. Every day you work in a different location with a different photographer and a different client."

Advertising work pays better than fashion, which sounds fine until you realize most advertising gigs require naturalistic makeup. The wild, exuberant stuff Sabrina loves to do has to stay screwed down in a jar most days.

The Freelance Life

Sabrina is a freelance makeup artist, a hired brush. Like all freelancers, she needs to find her own work. She has to promote herself, introduce herself to influential people in her field, and continually develop skills to stay marketable.

She lands her gigs through her own marketing, but her bookings are funneled through an agency in Toronto, one of only three in the city. For 15 percent of her earnings the agency does her billings, puts her work on its website, negotiaties her rate of pay, chases after the occasional late payer, and affords her the professional prestige of being represented by a respected agency. She strongly believes that clients are more likely to hire her because a good agency represents her. Nevertheless, she doesn't sit at home waiting for the agency to call. "I put myself out there to find work. Why would anyone care about my career more than I do?"

And that's the hard part—calling up photographers and ad agencies to ask if they'll take a look at her portfolio, or "book," as it is called in the business—a collection of photographs showing a stylist's work. "I am out there calling people, showing my portfolio, making phone calls, marketing myself. Sometimes it's hard to get people to meet with you. They're busy and you just have to be persistent."

Once her foot is in the door, the going gets even tougher. "It's nerve-wracking having people look at your book—like being on a blind date."

Sabrina no longer needs to go on blind dates personally or professionally, but she figures she's got another year to go before she has enough repeat and referral business to keep her as busy as she would like to be.

Much of her marketing involves visiting photographers'

studios with her book in tow. This is called a "go-see," as in "go see someone."

"I got booked for Monday from one of the go-sees last week. It was a BMW car ad. I had to do natural makeup and make them look like they were glistening from working out," Sabrina explains. When the work comes, the money is good. "I make in eight hours what I used to make in thirty selling cosmetics."

Sabrina frankly admits that a lot depends on who you know in her business. Who you know might get you in, she notes, but your personality and work ethic are what keep the door swinging open. "A lot of your jobs depend on your reputation. If you're not nice to people, you will not get work as easily."

Some people ply their personal connections too strongly and do themselves more damage than good, she's observed. "If you get a break, you can climb very quickly. Sometimes you can climb faster than your ability or maturity." For now, she's content with building her clientele one job at a time.

The Artist as a Young Girl

Sabrina grew up in Barrie, Ontario, a small town north of Toronto. You can't blame her for thinking her dad's salon and her aunt's aesthetics studio were fun places to hang out. While her aunt did manicures and pedicures, or the makeup for an entire bridal party, prepubescent Sabrina played with the makeup, learned to blend the colors, and became good at doing her friends' makeup. "I really took to it. It was just like paint. Once I even did a painting with makeup on paper."

Her aunt, with something of the avant-garde in her, too, started carrying MAC cosmetics early on in the famous Canadian brand's history. The line is known for its dramatic colors and high-end quality. Sabrina learned the MAC line watching her aunt make her clients beautiful. Meanwhile, small-town boredom was creeping up on her. "I needed to be where things were happening 24-7. There's always somebody weirder than you in a big city."

So at age nineteen, to experience the big city life, she jumped a plane to London, England, and moved in with a cousin. A year later, at her mother's insistence, she came home to enroll in a university drama program, for lack of a better choice. She discovered pretty quickly that acting wasn't for her.

"I just wanted to do the hair and makeup!" she says, thinking back on those unhappy days. She switched to a general arts program and lasted out the year, but afterward moved back to London to live with friends she had made.

Lucky enough to have European citizenship through her parents, Sabrina landed a job at the MAC cosmetic counter at the big department store Selfridges, in the heart of London's upscale shopping district. Because she had known the cosmetic line from its beginning, and because of her obvious enthusiasm, she was hired to sell makeup and do makeup application. The job paid an hourly wage instead of being commissioned based, which suited the intrepid traveler well, because she has always felt uncomfortable, she says, "selling things people don't need for my own benefit."

The MAC staff welcomed her warmly. Sabrina was particularly impressed with their pro team, a group of senior artists who came around at least once a week to instruct them in new techniques. "They sat us down right there at one of the stations and used one of us as a demo. Every three months we did a training session at the head office or at a hotel for a day, where we learned new trends, techniques, products, customer service skills, and so on," says Sabrina. "They grade you and give you pointers about the protocol, how to be hygienic, treat the person with respect, and follow their system. It is a great company to work for."

After a year behind the counter, Sabrina was determined to fast-forward her career by getting more intensive training on her own. Wanting to be nearer her family, too, she returned to Toronto and enrolled in Complections International, a makeup school. The eight-week course cost about Can$6,000—more than what a year in an arts program would cost at a Canadian university. Two weeks were given over to hair and six to fashion and photographic makeup. Out of sixteen students in her class, most of whom were from outside Canada, Sabrina scored the highest marks. "People did not take it seriously, nor did they have a passion for it, a creative vision," she says. "You can make a lot of money in this career, but [the other students] didn't have the focus. I was the only person to get 100 percent on the final exam." Frequent shoots with a good photographer were an integral part of the program so that students could leave with a small portfolio. At the end of eight weeks, Sabrina had the beginnings of a book.

Jobs, Books, and Bookings

After a few months of unemployment, the young graduate was hired by Calvin Klein cosmetics at the high-profile Holt Renfrew store in downtown Toronto. "I ran the counter on my own and had a few other people for my days off. I did the inventory, the cash, everything. I even organized a national event."

Unfortunately, that position was commission-based, an arrangement Sabrina didn't feel entirely comfortable with, so after six months she took a salaried job at the flagship MAC store on Bloor Street in Toronto, right beside the famous jewelery store, Tiffany's. She stayed there two and a half years, soaking up the training, loving the eccentric people, and serving actors and socialites. "The people at MAC became my family," she says warmly.

On her days off she was also trying to build her book by arranging "creatives"—sessions in which a photographer, model, clothing stylist, and makeup artist work together for free to get photographs they can all use to promote themselves. Sabrina got the ball rolling by looking in the phone book for the photographers who shot her work at Complections. She called other photographers, too, and sent them her business card, which was nothing if not memorable. "It had one of the makeup looks that I did at school, a close-up of my friend with blond dreadlocks—orange and pink shimmery shadow, over the top, crazy, nothing natural."

It worked, because a few photographers called her back.

She also had some help from her boyfriend, who hires photographers in his position as a graphic designer. "He got a few top guys to do a few sets with me, which was really great. I got a few pictures that were just so beautiful. The quality of the photo makes your work look good or bad."

With the start of a decent book and lots of networking with photographers and stylists, Sabrina started getting some gigs, which she scrambled to accommodate with her hours at MAC. One of her first freelance jobs was a high-profile AIDS campaign. Later, when one of the top photographers in Toronto offered her work, she gave MAC two weeks' notice. Family or not, Sabrina was committed to doing makeup more than selling it.

Not long after, with her book bulging with stunning photos, she bravely approached two agencies that represent makeup artists in Toronto. "Judy Inc. took me on right then and there," says Sabrina proudly. She's been with them since September 2003. Having representation is no guarantee of work, however. Sabrina is competing with fifteen other makeup and hair artists who are represented by the same agency. The quality and diversity of her book have to stand up well against the competition, even from within the agency. Sabrina leaves nothing to chance. Go-sees and creatives fill the gaps in her schedule and will do so until those gaps disappear.

At the end of the day Sabrina says, "I love my job and I'm good at it." That love and confidence impel her to keep promoting herself to find new and challenging work, upgrade her knowledge, and build influential contacts. Someone who used to dress to get attention now gets noticed by how well she "does up" others, and what once made her different is now making a difference.

EVERYTHING NEEDS A STYLIST, NOT JUST HEADS

Food, gardens, homes, pets, you name it—if it needs to look good for an ad, there's an artist or a stylist for it. There's even a professional association for people in this unusual line of work, called the Association of Stylists and Coordinators (www.stylistsasc.com).

Because of the clever deception that goes into food shots, food styling is a particularly interesting subspeciality. The site Career Prospects in Virginia offers an excellent description of food styling and the background needed to break into it. Here's a tantalizing behind-the-scenes peek:

> *The scoop of chocolate ice cream advertised on television is often not ice cream at all but tinted mashed potatoes. Real ice cream would melt under the cameraman's harsh lights. And the deliciously thick syrup poured on pancakes? It's probably motor oil.*
>
> —www3.ccps.virginia.edu/career_prospects/briefs/E-J/FoodStylists.shtml

SALARIED OR FREELANCE

Artists and stylists, whatever their speciality, are not necessarily freelancers. They may be employed by magazines or production companies, though the competition for these jobs is fierce. Most people who become stylists have extensive experience in the underlying field. For instance, food stylists are often chefs and interior stylists are interior decorators. In general, styling is a field for people with considerable work experience, but successful stylists may hire assistants.

SABRINA'S WORK ONLINE

Check out Sabrina Rinaldi's portfolio at her agent's site, www.judyinc.com. Notice the variety of artists this agency represents—hair, makeup, fashion and wardrobe, props, roomset, food, and others. You can find more portfolios online by Googling "stylist + agency." Sabrina's favorite makeup artist is Frances Hathaway. You can see her astonishing work at www.jumpmanagement.com.

The site www.rasource.com lists artists associated with print photography, along with their agencies.

FOR MORE ON MAKEUP PROGRAMS

Many community colleges offer makeup programs. Schools dedicated to teaching makeup, like Toronto's Complections, may also teach special-effects makeup for the movie industry. Film schools also teach special-effects makeup.

SABRINA'S BOOK RECOMMENDATIONS

Two of Sabrina's favorites are *Face Forward* and *Making Faces,* both written by Kevyn Aucoin and published by Little, Brown, in 2001 and 1999, respectively.

Never Forget a Contact

RYAN McCALLUM

PRO SPORT GENERAL MANAGER

"I had no players, no gym to play in, no staff, no office, no nothing. I was *it*," says Ryan McCallum about his first day as general manager of the yet-to-be-formed Tennessee Fury women's professional basketball team.

"That was kind of a shock. It usually takes a year to set up a pro team. I started on November first and the first game was February second. Having three months to set up a pro team is unheard of."

But, as he showed, not impossible. That year the Tennessee Fury came in second in the National Women's Basketball League (NWBL) and Ryan was named the pro league's executive of the year. The teams of the NWBL play in the

Women's National Basketball Association's (WNBA) off season. The distinction of being selected team executive of 2003 for the six-team league was all the sweeter because of Ryan's age. At twenty-four he was half as old as the other general managers in the league and younger than many of the players on his team. Not bad for somebody who only three years before had been slinging cold drinks and hot dogs to fans at basketball and hockey games.

In those critical first three months with the Tennessee Fury, Ryan had to set up an office, build a website, organize a press conference, find a coach, start a booster club, hire the players, find accommodations for the players, book a gym, get corporate sponsorship, order uniforms, and stay within the budget set by the team's owner. That would be a daunting job for even the most grizzled general manager, but Ryan's inexperience worked in his favor.

Recalling his telephone job interview, Ryan says, "I thought maybe I'd be some sort of media assistant, but when the league president called back to say they were considering me for the general manager job, I was like, 'OK, why not?'"

Somebody should have told him why not.

Overcoming the Fear of Being the Boss Man

"There is no such thing as a nine-to-five workday for me anymore," Ryan says. "It is at least ten to twelve hours a day, seven days a week." Though the workload never intimidated him, something else did. "The thing that scared me the most," he confesses, "was meeting the players. They're these big women and I'm in charge of them. Who wants to listen to a little guy who is younger than you? That was my biggest fear going in."

Ryan says he enjoys dealing with the players now, but there was a lot of razzing at the beginning, most of it good-natured. "The girls on the team would say, 'Get off the court! This ain't no hockey rink!' I used to shoot around with them in practice, but they made fun of me too much. They said I shoot like a girl."

At five foot eleven, Ryan has another guilty confession: he never, ever played basketball before starting the Fury.

Knowing His Strengths & Weaknesses

"I was really into hockey," Ryan explains. He played organized hockey from kindergarten to the end of high school. He also played lacrosse, soccer, and baseball, but he says frankly he was never the best player in any of them. "A lot of my friends were playing on the city rep teams, the best of the best. On a good day, I was average. I knew early on I wasn't going to the NHL, but I loved sports and knew I had to do something different."

Ryan started doing something different in his last year of high school when he got a job working Friday through Sunday selling refreshments at Toronto Raptors and Maple Leaf games in downtown Toronto, a job that required a forty-five-minute train ride into the city from his home in the burbs.

Between his own sports activities and work, Ryan was cruising through high school on neutral until he learned about sport management through a school presentation by college representatives that he was required to attend. He shifted into gear to qualify and was accepted to study sport management at Brock University in St. Catharines, Ontario, a small city just a few miles from the border of New York State.

Ryan continued his job selling refreshments at hockey and basketball games in Toronto through his first two years at Brock. His commute from St. Catharines to Toronto was an hour and a half each way.

A Pivotal Exchange Program

In his third year at Brock, Ryan participated in an international exchange program with the University of Tennessee, which also offers sport management. While there, Ryan became an intern with the Knoxville Speed of the United Hockey League. Interns generally work for free in exchange for experience and maybe a season's ticket. Many sports and media companies offer these positions and, despite the absence of pay, they are highly coveted jobs and difficult to land.

"Anything relating to the media was my job," Ryan recalls of his time with the Knoxville Speed. "I did everything, from updating the website and writing press releases to calling local media before and after games and keeping track of stats during the period for the broadcaster. I did it all. At the minor league level you can get a feel for everything and wear lots of hats."

Internships Don't Come Easy

After his year in Tennessee, Ryan returned for his final year at Brock University, where he was required to do a stint as an intern. The media experience with Knoxville, his job selling drinks and dogs in Toronto, and his unquenchable ambition led him to apply for the much-sought-after internship with Maple Leaf Sports and Entertainment, the company that owns the Raptors and the Maple Leafs.

"It was a long drive in for a trip up an elevator and a ten-minute interview," Ryan recalls. "The interview process was pretty intense. I walked out of there wondering how I had done and if I was sweating too much." Then he sat at home for three days wondering if he should e-mail his interviewer or call him to find out what was going on. "I finally e-mailed him," Ryan says. "'Yeah, we'll get back to you,' I was told. I waited a few more days, then they said to come in the next week for another interview. I did. Then another wait. After three and a half weeks they told me on a Thursday, 'You'll start on Monday.'

"I know a big part of getting Maple Leaf Entertainment to look at me was being employed for them selling food and beverages. I did the grunt work and busted my butt for three years so I could finally get noticed by some human resources person," says Ryan.

As an intern he was assigned to the New Media Sales Department, where he was responsible for selling ads and sponsorship deals for the company's website and for the new digital TV stations set up for the teams. Normally internships last only one semester, but Ryan wanted to keep his foot in the door and asked to stay on just one day a week for a second semester. "I was told the company had a stack of hundreds and hundreds of intern resumes, all people who were willing to work five days a week." Nevertheless, Ryan was able to stay on one day a week for the next semester, and when he graduated with a degree in sport management, he had an impressive résumé and enviable experience with a pro-sports team.

Contacts, Skills, & Exploiting Opportunities

Next, the hunt was on for a permanent position. "One thing I learned way back with the media in my first internship is that it's really important to keep in touch with all your contacts. Every month or so I called everyone, especially one of my profs from Tennessee, because I knew he had set up his students with so many great jobs. I bugged him until he forwarded my name to a new league that was coming to Knoxville." That league was the National Women's Basketball League, and the new team was to be the Tennessee Fury.

"At my first press conference [for the Fury], some of the press guys were laughing at me because I used to be sitting with them in my first job as an intern and now I was the one doing the talking," Ryan says, laughing.

"People skills are real big," he emphasizes. "It's not a desk job." General managers have to drum up corporate sponsorships by rubbing elbows with high-powered executives, get chummy with the sports press, and greet fans like they are your best friends.

But people skills aren't everything. "Computer skills are huge," says Ryan. He uses e-mail, updates the team website, writes press releases in Word, tracks team expenses in Excel, and puts together presentations for sponsors on PowerPoint. "You are lost without computer skills."

And the pay? Ryan says he's making good money. He is paid a base salary and gets a cut on all tickets sold and all sponsorship deals he signs. Money from those sources can far exceed his base salary.

For fun, Ryan still likes to slap the puck around. Once a week he plays with a league in Tennessee. "They think I'm some great secret from Canada," he says of the southern players whose skills generally aren't up to Canadian standards. "I'm a superstar down here, but if any of my Canadian friends were here it would be ridiculous."

The lure of hockey still pulls strong. Ultimately Ryan

would like to be general manager of the Toronto Maple Leafs, one of Canada's top hockey teams. Not long ago, a human resources person with the Leafs told him there was a GM opening. "In a few years, maybe," he says good-humoredly, as though the possibility is too remote to think about.

But Ryan is a guy who has made every opportunity count. He built networks of people who could help him. He went after a strategic job in high school and used it to get a highly competitive internship. He didn't bide his time in college just to get a degree; he pursued a program that helped launch him into the sports world, and he took advantage of an exchange program that power-boosted his ambitions. "Make the best of all situations and the good breaks will start to come," he says. General manager of the Toronto Maple Leafs? Before Ryan has too many more hats in his closet, likely.

One Year Later

If Ryan's experience is anything to judge by, the career of a sport manager can be as slippery as a wet football. After his success with the Fury, the owner of the Houston Stealth, another team in the league, asked him to take over.

"They were spending a bunch of money on players and they were winning, but there was nobody at their games and no sponsors," says Ryan. "I had to basically give the organization a facelift." He went in during the off season to raise the team's profile. Then, owing to an administrative oversight, his work visa expired, forcing him to return to Canada. He was ready to go home to try his luck back in Toronto.

Ryan sent his résumé to the president and CEO of the Toronto Argonauts. During his first interview with the president, he was hired on the spot to manage the team's corporate sponsorship, a position he believes plays to his strongest points as a general manager.

It was anything but a slam dunk. The year before, the Argos had declared bankruptcy, which scared away a good many sponsors. "For the first three months I was calling people and they were laughing at me," Ryan recalls somewhat painfully. "The season before, we had $300,000 in total sponsorship dollars. My goal was to personally bring in $250,000.

"It's one thing to be down in the U.S. with sponsorship as one of your roles and doing it on a part-time basis, but once you're in the big city dealing with big corporations and men double my age wondering why this young guy was trying to persuade them to spend $100,000 to put a patch on a jersey, it opened up a whole new world to me. It was crazy but I loved it."

Ryan says he raised nearly $700,000, almost three times his assigned goal, and he raked in a considerable amount of money in commissions to supplement his salary. He was looking forward to taking a month off, traveling to Europe, then signing the sponsors again. "I had brought on twenty new sponsors, ready to go all over again," he says.

"Sponsorship is all about the relationship," he observes. "I built relationships with a ton of different people."

Those good relationships included the one with his boss, so when the president of the Argos told Ryan he was fired, he laughed, thinking it was a joke. Unfortunately, it wasn't. A new office manager was going to do corporate sponsorship differently, and without Ryan's services. Despite the shock and feelings of betrayal, however, Ryan responded professionally. "I made a point of saying I wanted to make sure we were leaving on good terms, and I shook his hand."

Because Ryan keenly appreciates the value of networking and relationships, he's learned not to burn bridges. "If you get on somebody's bad side you are going to have a lot of enemies; just because you're right doesn't mean it's your way or the highway."

Not surprisingly, Ryan has landed on his feet because of his extensive network. A contact Ryan met while working for the Argos offered him a job as soon as he learned Ryan was available. So within two months of being sacked, Ryan became manager of Corporate Partnership—a high-ranking corporate sponsorship job for Molson Sports and Entertainment in Toronto. It's also the best money yet.

Ryan's ultimate goal is to be president and CEO of a major sports operation. Given the seeming impermanence of jobs in the sports world, he makes a point of keeping in touch with many of his former contacts, even those in Tennessee, which now must seem a world away. "Relationships are huge," he emphasizes. He's kept a spreadsheet of every company and person he's contacted since he graduated. "A lot of times I've had opportunities jump up at me just from touching base."

Some day, probably not too long from now, one base he touches will deliver him to home plate.

NO WAYNE GRETZKY BUT A SPORTS NUT ANYHOW?

There's a lot more to sports than the athletics. To move from the stands to the sidelines, consider getting involved with a booster club. Booster clubs are for sports teams what fan clubs are for celebrities, but with the possibility of occasionally doing odd jobs for the team. Every sports team has a booster club. You can reach a team's booster club through the team's website, or try www.sportsfansofamerica.com/links/boosterclubs/main1.htm for a listing of football, baseball, and hockey booster clubs. Joining a booster club is free, and it not only shows your support for the team, but is a great way to get to know the team and its workings.

If you've got a little more time on your hands, not-for-profit sports organizations like the local kids' soccer league are always looking for volunteers. This could be an opportunity to gain some management experience.

SPORT MANAGEMENT PROGRAMS

Sport management is becoming a popular offering at American colleges, but you can also find it at a smaller number of universities in other countries, including Canada and Australia.

At www.nassm.com, the North American Society for Sport Management (NASSM), an organization for sport management academics, has an extensive database of academic institutions around the world offering sport management programs.

NETWORK CONNECTIONS

Ryan is a master networker. He excels at building contacts with people and then turning *their* contacts into his own. To be a good networker you have to find accessible people in your area of interest, put yourself in front of them, and be prepared with a snappy summary of your interests and how these people can help. You may be surprised to find that most people want to help teens who have smarts and ambition, but you have to help others understand exactly what it is you want them to assist with.

Many personal networking organizations and websites require a registration fee, so it is probably best to see how far you can develop your networking skill on your own, perhaps with the help of a library book, and a spreadsheet or contact management database. Keeping well-organized contact information is a must.

And, of course, know when to take no for an answer. As they say in sales, every no gets you closer to a yes.

OTHER SPORT MANAGEMENT ASSOCIATIONS

Besides NASSM, there's the European Association for Sport Management (EASM) at www.easm.net and the Sport Management Association of Australia and New Zealand (SMAANZ) at www.griffith.edu.au/school/gbs/tlhs/smaanz.

If you're interested in raising sponsorships for sports organizations, as Ryan is doing, try the Sport Marketing Association at www.sportmarketingassociation.com.

BOOKS & MAGAZINES

Street & Smith's SportsBusiness Journal is *the* industry resource, at www.sportsbusinessjournal.com. Good books on sport management include *On the Ball: What You Can Learn about Business from America's Sports Leaders,* written by D. Carter and D. Rovell and published by FT Prentice Hall in 2003; *You Can't Play the Game If You Don't Know the Rules: Career Opportunities in Sports Management,* by D. Carter, published by Impact in 1994; *Career Opportunities in the Sports Industry,* by S. Field, published by Checkmark Books in 1999; and *The Business of Sports,* by S. Rosner and K. Shropshire, published by Jones and Bartlett in 2004.

Thanks for these recommendations go to Cheri Bradish, professor of sport management at Brock University.

Turning Love to Liberation

AMY BENNETT

ASSISTANCE DOG TRAINER

"I like helping to give people freedom," says Amy Bennett, a young woman who has managed to combine her love of animals with a particularly meaningful occupation. Amy breeds and trains dogs to help children with autism and adults with mobility problems. Since she began New Hope Assistance Dogs in 2002, her business has placed nine intensively trained dogs with paraplegics, quadriplegics, and autistic children.

Having trouble getting your dog to shake a paw? Assistance dogs know between eighty and a hundred commands, and when they're in action, their skills are awesome. "They turn on and off light switches, open and close doors. They can be taught to help someone who is paralyzed roll over in bed, take laundry out of the dryer, or put it into the washer. They can retrieve, open fridge doors and get things out—any number of things," says Amy.

With about forty dogs of various ages under four years old to choose from, Amy can match each client with a dog best suited to his or her personality. "We'll give a more outgoing dog to an individual who likes to get out and do stuff," says Amy. "Somebody who's more laid back, we give a quieter dog. Our best dogs go to the kids. These dogs have to be nurturing, very gentle, tolerant, because kids are unpredictable. You don't know if they might grab the dog's ear, pull the dog's tail, climb on them. The dog needs to be able to take it in stride."

Young children are generally not given access to assistance dogs because of concerns about the reliability of the dog's feeding, grooming, and general care, but Amy is a passionate advocate for the early pairing of special needs children with assistance dogs. "We've seen the miracles of placing a dog with a three-year-old child," says the twenty-three-year-old trainer emphatically. Amy credits a dog she trained with saving the life of an autistic child by pulling him unconscious from a flooded pit.

Because of the dog's aid and companionship, "that child went from being violent, nonverbal, and out of control to being gentle and friendly," says Amy. "He speaks now, though not fluently, and isn't aggressive anymore. He is now able to go to regular kindergarten because he has a dog with him, instead of being in a special class." He sings his alphabet to the dog, too.

How It Began

Amy always had animals when she was growing up in northwestern Pennsylvania. "I got my very own pony when I was three," she says, with pride. "My sister and I used to take Frosty down to the local nursing home for [outdoor] parties. We let people pet him and we gave visiting relatives rides."

The idea for the pony rides came from a friend of Amy's mother who worked in the nursing home. She knew about the gentle Shetland pony with the big white fluffy mane and tail who invited himself into Amy's kitchen to eat sugar cookies off the counter. Amy agreed to bring Frosty to the nursing home because it was a familiar place to her: she often went there to sing while her mother played guitar for the residents. Those fun pony rides turned out to be the beginning of Amy's lifelong devotion to animals and to people in need.

Later, when she was seven, Amy got a pet Dutch rabbit whom she named Lilac and trained to walk on a leash. She took Lilac to the nursing home, too, only this critter could sit on people's laps and be petted by adoring elderly people (with a towel draped on their laps in case Lilac had an accident, which fortunately, she never did).

At twelve years old, Amy used her babysitting money to buy her own golden retriever puppy directly from a local breeder. She picked the biggest puppy in the litter and named him Shadow because he followed her everywhere.

"From there," Amy says, "I did all his obedience training, went to different classes, and read tons of books on how to train dogs, and I got him certified as a therapy dog." Shadow was one and Amy was thirteen.

A therapy animal is a specially trained pet that visits patients in hospitals, nursing homes, schools, and other places where petting, playing, and having the companionship of an animal can be healing. To qualify as a therapy dog, Shadow had to have a health screening, a temperament test, and obedience tests. The tests are conducted by representatives of a certified pet therapy program, a program Amy learned about from the instructor of the obedience classes she attended with Shadow.

Shadow visited hospitals, nursing homes, and rehabilitation centers. "He's very good at his job," says Amy. "Sometimes people resist at first, mostly because they're told they have to do this as part of therapy. We had one particular gentleman who sat with his arms folded and didn't want to do anything. Shadow sat next to him for a while and then seemed to say, 'That's it, you're going to pat me.' So he took his nose and kept pushing it under the gentleman's hand, pushing and pushing until the man couldn't stop grinning and he began patting Shadow and hugging him. Shadow does things like that just on his own."

Pioneering Her Own Program

Therapy dogs can bring withdrawn and sad people out of their shell, and a lot more. Part of Amy's mission has been to educate program administrators about the recuperative benefits of therapy dogs.

Another friend of Amy's mother was a physical therapist at a rehabilitation hospital in New York State. She wanted Amy to start a program there but New York had never before had a therapy dog program in a healthcare facility. "I was fourteen then," recalls Amy. "I said yes to the idea, but I didn't know what I was getting into. It was a lot of work initially because the therapists didn't understand the best way to let the dogs interact with the patients. They wanted to direct the interaction and would say things like 'Pat the dog ten times.' They had Shadow lie on a table, and they'd bring the patients up in wheelchairs to brush him and that was the end of it.

"That didn't seem like much fun for anybody, so I did more research on therapy dogs and wrote a letter to the head of the department at the hospital explaining the different things I wanted to do with my dog to better utilize his skills and incorporate them into the patients' therapy. We went round and round, and after a while they let me do whatever I wanted."

By now Amy had a second golden retriever, Pilgrim, also a certified therapy dog. "I could play fetch with the dogs," says Amy. "We'd go out into the hallway and the patients would throw a ball or soft toy, and that would get them using their arms. I was working primarily with people who had had a stroke or a traumatic brain injury; they needed to get moving. I had trained Shadow to take one step and then stop so he could easily walk next to patients who were using a walker. They were able to hold on to his leash and walk him themselves. It may not seem significant, but it was to them. Shadow was trained with voice commands and hand signals so I could control him as though I had him myself."

Amy brought in photo albums so the patients could see Shadow and Pilgrim as puppies. By this time the patients adored the dogs and loved every minute of working with them. "We had several people light up and start talking for the first time [since their strokes]," recounts Amy.

After a year and a half of working at the rehabilitation hospital, Amy was asked to expand her program to the adolescent behavioral health unit. This unit cares for children from two to eighteen years old with behavioral issues.

"I saw a kid go from being scared to death of people, just sitting on the floor crying, to being curled up between the dog's legs, sleeping, because she felt so safe. Kids who hadn't been making much progress in their therapy or who weren't going to get to go home for a couple of weeks would start working with the dogs and have a complete transformation."

Shadow and Pilgrim even played a role in encouraging the kids to read. Amy brought in books with pictures of different dog breeds and the children learned to read the breed names.

"We took the dogs outside and I taught the kids basic dog care, grooming, a little bit of training; they would just open right up. Kids would write me cards and make little gifts for the dogs. That was a really neat experience."

Training for Herself

Amy did animal therapy work for four years, without any pay, until she was out of high school. "I wanted to continue doing the work but on a deeper level and make a living doing it," she says. Amy had learned about the Assistance Dog Institute from a small ad at the back of *Dog Fancy* magazine. Shadow and Pilgrim were left to spend some quality time with Amy's parents while she used the education money her grandparents had set aside for her to fly to Santa Rosa, California, and attend a one-year program to qualify as an assistance dog trainer instructor.

"We had probably seventy-five dogs there," she recalls of her college year. "We studied psychology so we knew how to work with the patients. We raised and trained the dogs and placed them with clients who came for two weeks so we could train them to work with the dogs. Then we would do follow-up on the placement. It was a very in-depth and thorough program, so when I came back from California I was able to get my program started here."

Breaking Out on Her Own, with Patience

Amy had a few reasons for wanting to start her own training school. She wanted to stay in her rural corner of Pennsylvania, and there weren't any assistance dog training organizations anywhere near her home to employ her. She also wanted to specialize in working with children. "Most organizations don't place dogs with kids as young as I do," observes Amy, so the decision to start her own business was an obvious one. The Santa Rosa school she had attended gives out seed grants to help their graduates start up their own programs. With this money, Amy was able to buy her first litter of yellow Lab puppies—thirteen of them, born on the kitchen floor of her home, which is set on fifteen acres of land. Grants from other sources followed in addition to her own fundraising activities, which still help keep her afloat, but as more dogs are trained and placed with owners, a more independent stream of income is developing. Her spacious property, bought with her husband when they were married in 2001, is a great asset to her business, with plenty of room for kennels and romping space.

For the first few years of her business, this committed trainer and the dozen or so others who work with her part-time to train the dogs, play with the puppies, work in the office, and do fundraising went without pay. The money they earned from selling the trained dogs went back into providing food and care for the next generation of assistance dogs. Recently, Amy has been able to pay herself and her trainers a modest wage. She is confident that with more time and greater awareness of her program, she will be able to support herself and some of her trainers as well as other assistance dog training centers do.

Amy is now the mother of two young children. Asked if she has had moments of discouragement in establishing her business, she says, "I could never give it up. It is in my heart." Her animals just may share her feelings. Frosty, now in his late twenties and blind, is living in a lush southern state helping disabled children learn how to ride. Amy has harnessed her love to help liberate people from the restrictions of their disabilities. Perhaps the same could be said of her animals, whose love and devotion have given freedom and new hope to their most grateful human companions.

CONTRIBUTING THROUGH YOUR OWN BUSINESS

Amy started her own assistance dog training business so she could play a part in pioneering the use of assistance dogs with young children while living where she wanted to live. Starting your own business is a big step, but it can be the easiest way to accomplish something that might be more difficult some other way. Financing, accounting, taxes, hiring, and all the other things that go into making a business can seem towering obstacles to the uninitiated. But that shouldn't stop anyone with a unique and important skill.

Amy's business is not-for-profit, which means that her business must serve the public interest. Non-profit organizations are often eligible for grants from government and charities, and they have a different tax status from for-profit businesses. Except for these differences, non-profit businesses must be run just like any other business. Salaries must be paid, customers must be satisfied, and success depends on how well the business is run. Salaries are generally lower in not-for-profit businesses, but they need not be and can be comparable to similar jobs in for-profit businesses.

Whether you want to start a business for profit or for the public interest, resources abound to help you. Finding money to get a business off the ground may not be as hard as you think. Sure, banks are tough, but well-off community-minded citizens can often fill the financing breach if they believe you have the personal and professional stuff to launch and sustain a successful enterprise. Not-for-profit businesses have a slight advantage in that they can pursue grants.

To get from the idea to the presentation stage, one of your first resources should be your school's Junior Achievement program. Now established worldwide, this program was started in the United States to encourage entrepreneurism in elementary and high school students.

After that, check out the website of the U. S. Small Business Administration (www.sba.gov/starting_business/index.html). The SBA site explains just about everything you will need to know about starting a business, and has a great section for young entrepreneurs. Another government site, usgovinfo.about.com/library/weekly/blstategrants.htm, offers state-by-state information on small business grants and other financial assistance available at the state level. For information on starting a non-profit business, see nonprofit.about.com.

Don't be afraid to seek out a mentor. Many businesspeople would love the chance to share their knowledge with someone young and ambitious. You don't necessarily need someone who works in a field related to your enterprise either, though it would help. Business skills are fairly transferable. The important thing is to find someone who takes you seriously, respects you, and will give you solid advice based on his or her experience. A knowledgeable mentor will be able to guide you to potential sources of financing, too. If you can't find a mentor through your personal network, you can contact SCORE at www.score.org. This nonprofit agency matches entrepreneurs with experienced businesspeople who volunteer as mentors.

All the information you need to make your mark with a business is out there for the taking. Overcoming the voice of worry inside your head may just be your biggest challenge.

AMY'S BOOK & MAGAZINE RECOMMENDATIONS

Most reasonably large libraries have a wide selection of books and magazines about dogs, working dogs, and dog training. Amy's personal favorites are *Good Owners, Great Dogs,* by Brian Kilcommons and Sarah Wilson, published by Warner Books in 1992; and *Dog Perfect: The User-Friendly Guide to a Well-Behaved Dog,* by Sarah Hodgson, published by Wiley in 2003; and the magazine *Dog Fancy* (www.dogfancy.com).

VOLUNTEERING

Visit the pound. Your local Society for the Prevention of Cruelty to Animals (SPCA) may be looking right now for energetic folks to clean the kennels, exercise the dogs, groom the cats, and pet the gerbils.

Assist a dog trainer. This may mean nothing more than toting and hauling gear to and from classes, but you'll get to see and hear how a professional works.

Become a foster parent. Assistance dogs need to be socialized when they are puppies, which means they have to live with a loving family until they are old enough to start their formal training. Assistance Dogs of America Inc. provides an excellent online description of the tasks involved in socializing a dog for its program, and extends an open invitation to volunteers. Check out adai.org; under "Get Involved," go to "Become a Foster Family."

If fostering a puppy is too ambitious for the other members of your household, try calling up the assistance dog training school nearest you to ask what else you can do to help. The school may hold an open house or give demonstrations during the year. And volunteers generally have first crack at adopting retired or unsuitable dogs!

Make your own pet a therapy pet. Many nursing homes let people bring their pet in for the comfort of the residents as long as the pet is well behaved and is up-to-date with vaccinations. However, some nursing homes may require pets to be certified as a therapy animal. (Most other public institutions do require this certification.)

Volunteer at a kennel or a breeder's. You know what you'll be shoveling, but you'll have some very grateful fans.

Consider being an occasional companion to children and adults with disabilities so you become familiar with the kinds of assistance they need, and bring your pet along if she's polite.

GETTING YOUR PET CERTIFIED

The Delta Society (www.deltasociety.org) and Therapy Dogs International (www.tdi-dog.org) offer short courses in how to visit institutions with a pet, and they certify pets as therapy animals.

SHOWS, SCHOOLS, GEAR, & MORE

Dog shows and obedience trials. Shows and trials are listed in your local newspaper. You can also find listings though the nearest branch of the American Kennel Club (www.akc.org).

More advanced obedience competitions are sponsored by a large assortment of obedience and protection sporting associations, with odd-sounding names like French Ring and Schutzhund, that post their trials across the country.

North American Ring Association: www.ringsport.org. French Ringsport is a kind of obedience/protection competition developed in France. This site has links to many other dog obedience and protection sports.

Assistance Dogs International (www.adionline.org/service.html) lists many assistance dog training facilities, and has a member newsletter.

The American Working Dog Federation (www.awdf.net)

links to some out-of-the-ordinary organizations pertinent to working dogs, such as the Canine Accelerant Detection Association, Canine Sports Medicine, the Institute for Canine Forensics, and many others.

Wolf Packs (wolfpacks.com/serviced.htm) sells gear for dogs—not wolves. They list assistance dog resources, including schools, by state and country.

DOG TRAINING SCHOOLS

The Assistance Dog Institute (www.assistancedog.org) in Santa Rosa, California, offers a one- or two-year certification program for training assistance dogs.

Most if not all guide dog and assistance dog schools also train the trainers. Check out www.thepuppyplace.org, devoted to seeing eye and guide dog programs. The site's FAQ section provides detailed information on becoming a guide dog trainer.

About twenty-five schools in the United States train police and military dogs and offer instructor training as well. None of these are accredited by any organization. If you're seriously thinking of enrolling in a training program, you might want to follow the recommendations of Jerry Bradshaw, founder of Tarheel Canine Training, and

Tarheel Canine Sports Protection Association. He advises prospective students to research the accomplishments of a school's trainers, get references from graduates, and visit the school before deciding whether to enroll. Tarheel Canine Training also offers correspondence courses at www.tarheelcanine.com.

Comics, Video Games, & Raw Determination

MIKE KRAHULIK & JERRY HOLKINS

INTERNET COMIC STRIP CREATORS & VIDEO GAME REVIEWERS

Mike and Jerry are dorks, by their own admission. They met while working for their high school newspaper. Jerry wrote articles, Mike drew pictures. They played video games and made comics together. When they graduated they got dorky jobs—one serviced computers, the other sold them.

But in their hearts and in their spare time, they were caped comic book creators giving life to superheroes in chicken outfits and form to far-flung apocalyptic visions. Their homemade comic books were eight-page black-and-white beauties printed at Kinko's and sold in comic book stores in Spokane, Washington, for fifty cents each. They don't know if one ever sold. News flash: If you have one of these fifty-cent specials it's probably worth five hundred dollars because these guys are big—superfantastic, mega-galactic big. They're "Tycho" and "Gabe" of *Penny Arcade*. For those who just emerged from a germ bubble or are over thirty, www.penny-arcade.com is devoted to video game news and reviews and features a comic strip about two misanthropic young men, Tycho and Gabe, who play video games every conscious and semiconscious moment. Based on the number of unique hits *Penny Arcade's* site receives, the comic book duo estimate the strip is read by millions, including many rabidly loyal fans and everybody who's anybody in the gaming industry.

Tycho and Gabe are, of course, characters in the *Penny Arcade* strip. Their real-life foils are Jerry Holkins, twenty-nine, and Mike Krahulik, twenty-seven. Ask them if they had any idea six years ago that their strip would morph into this Internet hulk and they laugh. They came perilously close to being suits—once.

The Beginnings

After a few years of putting out their Kinko minis, Jerry and Mike created a comic for a contest in *Next Generation*

Magazine, a magazine about video games. This was the birth of *Penny Arcade*, but the rather edgy bundle of joy did not find a home at *Next Generation*. This rejection, however, didn't diminish Jerry and Mike's affection for their creation. Instead, they got a popular video game site, *Looney Games*, to host the comic.

"We did one strip a week and pretty soon we were getting a lot of e-mails, so we started doing two a week," says Mike. "When we had about twenty thousand readers, we decided to get our own website. That was in 1999, and now our readership is in the millions as best we can count it. It's a full-time job for both of us and a third guy who runs the business side." But they didn't rescue the princess without some setbacks.

One comic on a home page does not a website make, so Jerry, the writing half, started posting video game reviews to shrink the white space. With two comics a week and two reviews a week, the pair were feeling stretched. Remember, they were still punching a clock with their full-time jobs.

Well, this was 1999, the heyday of the Internet investment boom. Website aggregators were trolling the Web looking for sites they could link together and place advertising on. Mike and Jerry were approached by a company that offered them a steady income in exchange for placing ads on their website. *Penny Arcade* joined this aggregator and for a few months all went well; the ads were placed and they got a regular check. Mike and Jerry saw the specter of uninterrupted geekery before them. Mike quit his nine-to-five gig and got married. A few months later, Jerry quit his job as a technology support specialist with the Spokane Public Schools.

Bust

Although the ads on their site were generating enough money to support the two of them, they weren't living in splendor. Jerry's place was a rat-infested rental house whose construction quality he describes with his trademark cutting wit: "Imagine a man with a band saw and a few episodes of *This Old House*. He has no practical construction knowledge, but at the same time he has a deep desire and a power tool." It wasn't a castle, but it wasn't even home for very long. The dot-com boom was quickly followed by the dot-com bust and *Penny Arcade*'s cash cow suddenly and unexpectedly expired. Within three hours of finding out about their aggregator's bankruptcy, Jerry got evicted from his rental house.

So there they were, two guys with a high school education, no jobs, no income, both married, and one couple with no place to live. Their desolation was even greater because they no longer had the rights to *Penny Arcade*—the website or the printed form.

"We signed a contract saying we would be a part of them [the aggregator], but we didn't understand what we were doing," recalls Jerry. "We actually *sold Penny Arcade* to this company," he says with disbelief still in his voice.

As for the print rights, they had fooled those away in another crummy contract, this time with a publisher. In exchange for publishing *Penny Arcade*'s first book of collected comics, they had agreed to give the publisher the rights to their first five years of books. The idea was to publish one book of collected *PA* comics a year. It took a whole year for the first book to be printed. According to Mike, they were never paid and the publisher has moved and is no longer in touch with them but still retains the print rights.

Looking back on those bleak days, Jerry says, "I remember saying I didn't think I could carry on and this was probably it. I thought *Mike* was going to console *me* but we were both at the depths of despair."

Turnaround

But things turned quickly. Jerry and his wife were taken in by a compassionate entrepreneur who let them rent a room. The Web comic duo contacted a lawyer and regained the rights to the *Penny Arcade* website, a recovery made possible by the aggregator's collapse. Shortly after, Amazon contacted them with an idea that would put ramen on their tables for the next few years: the Amazon honor system, familiar to all who visit web comics today.

"Nobody else was doing anything like it at the time," says Mike. "We put a little button up that said, If you like *Penny Arcade,* please donate a few dollars a month. Thank goodness enough of our readers were donating that it supported us until advertising came back and Robert found us."

Robert is the business brain behind *Penny Arcade*. He was consulting for a South Korean video game company when he approached Mike and Jerry to buy some advertising from them on *Penny Arcade*. When the pair came back to him with a laughably small price tag of $1,500, Robert knew they didn't know the value of what they had built.

"We didn't know what it was worth," admits Mike. "But the fact is that at the time, like now, *Penny Arcade* was as big as or bigger, than a lot of the major video game websites."

Robert persuaded them to take him on without pay for a few months, and since then the donation button has come off and the site has been supporting three people full-time through advertising and an assortment of *Penny Arcade* merchandise.

Jerry and Mike are no longer working out of Mike's apartment; they've moved into a three-room office in a Seattle shopping mall. They've paid down their personal debt, and both of them have bought houses. And Mike has a baby he's named after his comic alter ego, Gabriel.

To Thine Own Self Be True

Mike believes when *Penny Arcade* started, there were only two other comic strips on the Internet. Now there are too many to count, but that doesn't mean there isn't room for more. If you're thinking you might want to add your heroes to that pack, Mike has some advice. "Create comics that you enjoy and don't listen to what other people tell you," he says. "We had plenty of people e-mailing us, saying our stuff wasn't good. Concentrate on doing what you like, and keep doing it. And stay on schedule. If you put your comic out on schedule, you'll keep getting readers. Miss a couple of days and people tend to drift away."

Jerry emphasizes the importance of using your own interests as a springboard for a creative career. "For a long time," he says, "we tried to create comics that we thought would fit in the marketplace—like the comics we had seen in stores. Certainly we were interested in them, but it wasn't our passion. We actually liked video games more than most other things, but for years we toiled on projects that didn't exactly turn our cranks because we didn't believe we could ever possibly do it this way. We make comics about video games. That's ridiculous on the face of it."

But not so ridiculous after all. Says Jerry, "You really can make art your living." He and Mike have done it, and their living gets more affluent every year. Two guys who just wanted to make comic strips have forged their own empire by combining cartooning, game reviews and webpublishing. It may seem an unlikely business model, but it has worked. In addition to having domination over Tycho and Gabe, these artists have a respected voice in the gaming industry and are above all masters of their own destinies, because they were faithful to their passion.

BE YOUR OWN MARVEL

Mike and Jerry might have been called comics bloggers if blogging had been around when they started. Any web-based publication with periodic installments is a blog, whether it involves comics, photographs, or written commentary. For most bloggers, self-expression is its own reward, but a lucky few develop big followings that lead to a book contract, a newspaper column, or a major standalone website. If there's something inside you that needs to get out, make the Internet your publisher. A good place to start is www.blogger.com, a site that makes blog entries simple enough for a sixty year old.

IS THERE A TOON IN YOUR HEART?

If you are interested in cartooning, you can design your own digital comic and post it on your own site and on other sites that are willing to display it or link to it. Are newspapers and magazines your target? Mike says to focus your efforts on publications with very specific interests that mirror your own: "If you love dogs, find a dog magazine and do cartoons about dogs that other dog lovers would appreciate." Don't overlook your school and local newspapers. After a few acceptances, you can shoot for bigger newspapers and magazines, but Mike cautions, "Keep a big collection of rejection letters, burn them in the winter to keep warm, and hope for the best." Mike much prefers the more direct route of the Internet, where "there's no editor standing in your way, nothing keeping you from having your comic online tomorrow."

EVEN SUPERHEROES NEED HELP SOMETIMES

With luck and persistence, you may be able to get feedback on your own work from exhibitors at comic conventions. Comic-Con International (www.comic-con.org), the largest comic convention, is held in San Diego every year. Many other shows are listed at www.comicbookconventions.com/conventions.htm, a site put together by a fan who must dream in dialogue bubbles. The best aspect of conventions is being able to see and hear comic creators in person.

Penny Arcade, by the way, has its own convention once a year just outside Seattle.

MORE ABOUT THE FUNNIES

For a classic guide to the making of comics, which is also a comic book itself, pick up a copy of *Understanding Comics: The Invisible Art*, by Scott McCloud, published by HarperCollins in 1993. *Reinventing Comics,* also by Scott McCloud, is about digital cartooning and its future; it was published by HarperCollins in 2000. *Toon Art: The Graphic Art of Digital Cartooning,* by Steven Withrow gives a brief history of cartooning, explains how to do digital cartoons, and offers many examples of digital cartoons and an outstanding "toon reference guide," with lists of websites and useful books. It was published in 2003 by Watson-Guptil.

Some cartooning books also give advice on selling your work. Two titles to look at are *The Everything Cartooning Book: Create Unique and Inspired Cartoons for Fun and Profit,* by Brad J. Guigar, published by Adams Media in 2004; and *The Complete Idiots Guide to Cartooning* by Arnold Wagner and Shannon Turlington, published in 2002 by Alpha.

GETTING HELP WITH CONTRACTS

At the beginning of their careers, Mike and Jerry knew nothing about legal contracts. They trusted the people they were dealing with and ended up regretting their ignorance.

Protect yourself. If someone is interested in buying your work, you should know it has value, and almost certainly more value than you will be offered during the first round of negotiation. To someone who is just starting out, hiring a lawyer seems a luxury as out of reach as a Mercedes. But you may be surprised by the generosity of lawyers, especially those who practice alone in their own firms. These sole practitioners have more flexibility with their time, and you just might be lucky to find one who is willing to help you for free, at least to read through your first contract. A lawyer can point out aspects of a contract that could be disadvantageous to you in the future, and can prevent you from inadvertently selling the rights to your work. Look under "Attorneys" in the Yellow Pages. Try calling a few who do not have large ads and who may work alone, because lawyers with large firms generally have less freedom to volunteer their time. Speak frankly about your situation and what you need. If you get help, be grateful, and remember that help when some brave and nervous young soul approaches *you* one day for advice. Keep the karma going!

Passion and Focus

ZOE LEARNER

ASTRONOMER & MARTIAN BACKSEAT DRIVER

Zoe Learner's signature is on Mars. Her grandmother's signature is on the moon. "I love thinking about that," admits Zoe. Like medieval craftsmen who carved their own portraits in the towering cathedrals they built, those who work with space machinery leave their signature on their creations.

"It's not quite as romantic as it sounds," says Zoe. "You don't actually get to go up [to the machines] with an etching pen and scratch your name in, because of sanitation reasons." Scientists are careful not to contaminate celestial bodies with earthly germs. Somewhere on the moon sits a canister with film of the signatures of those who worked on the Lunar Module project. On Mars, the signatures are in electronic form, digitalized and saved on a microchip that is tucked into the body of two intrepid robot vehicles over 300 million miles away from earth.

Zoe helps drive the Mars rovers from the (metaphorical) back seat. She's also a Ph.D. student in the astronomy department of Cornell University. Thirty-five years ago, Zoe's grandmother worked on the first rover to land on the moon. She was an engineer with a NASA subcontractor. Although her grandmother died when Zoe was just seven, it was her grandmother's occupation that made her own interests and career choice seem ordinary... to her.

Zoe has long had a passion for space science, and she has overcome significant obstacles with single-minded focus to pursue a career in astronomy. Anyone who dreams of a job in academia should pay heed to how Zoe did it. She is now among a team of scientists and engineers directing the activities of two very hardworking rovers that are examining the surface of Mars. The intrepid vehicles' mission is to find evidence of liquid water in the red planet's hoary past. There's plenty of ice on Mars, but evidence of water in liquid form at one time would mean that there had been at least one necessary condition for life as we know it on the planet.

Doing a Small Job Well

As a documentarian on the scientific team, Zoe is responsible for taking notes during meetings in which the scientists discuss the data they have received from the rovers and the tasks they want the rovers to perform on the basis of that data. She documents their instructions and must understand their objectives so when a question or ambiguity arises in their absence, she can direct the engineers who program the rovers in keeping with the scientists' intentions. The rovers call home only twice a day—once for data download and again for instruction upload. Engineers must program the rovers' moves a day in advance, because the distance is so great that real time instructions and continuous communication are not possible.

"We actually run through every single little step we are going to have the rover do," explains Zoe. "I'm one of many people who sit there to make sure it makes sense, that it is what [the] science [team] wants, that it makes sense engineering-wise, that the commands are in the right order. Then when everyone is happy about it, we approve the plan and it is ready to be uplinked, and I file a report."

Part of her job is to look over the shoulder of the engineers who write the commands that direct the rovers in their extraterrestrial investigations. The rovers' place of toil is a planet with pink air, red soil, and nighttime temperatures that plunge to minus one hundred degrees, with an atmosphere of nothing but carbon dioxide. "There are pictures I could point to and say I set up the commands for that picture," says the astronomer. You might think a lowly graduate student whose most exciting job is backseat driving wouldn't have much to contribute to a team of experienced astroscientists, but on occasion, her oversight has helped the team capture images they might have otherwise overlooked. She has also helped solve some problems.

"We were having the meeting, trying to decide what kinds of pictures to take," recalls Zoe. "One person wanted large pictures and another person noted that we don't have the data volume to take such big pictures—they would have to be smaller. But that wasn't acceptable for their needs. There was a conflict between what science wants and the resources available. I said, 'What if we took some of the images smaller but the important ones big?'"

That suggestion was adopted, and Zoe felt both gratified and encouraged. "That's why you have a big science team, because you never know who is going to have a way of making it work. I had a feeling of, hey, I did something!"

Mistakes: Part of Doing the Hard Stuff

Not all of Zoe's contributions have been stunning successes, and she's frank about that. "There were times when I messed up," she says. "We wanted to take a picture of a rock, and we were also using instruments on it from [the rover's] arm. To save time we try to do other things while we are using the arm—killing two birds with one stone. I suggested taking a picture while we were doing certain arm work, without it occurring to me that that was the rock we had the arm on. The next day we got back all these images of the backside of the arm, not the rock. Only then did I realize that I had taken the picture of the rock while we were blocking it with the arm. There was the initial feeling of 'Oh my God, I messed up!' but then there was the realization that we can take the image today and we'll make sure we move the arm out of the way."

Her error cost the rover some time and the engineers a little more work. Knowing how badly she felt about this, her academic adviser and the principal investigator for the science instruments on the rovers, Dr. Steve Squyres, pointed out to her that there had been twenty other people in the room and that nobody else had caught the error.

"I screwed up, but the world didn't end," Zoe says philosophically. "I didn't ruin the whole mission. It happens. Ever since that time, though, I always check: Is the arm out of the way?

"Messing up is part of doing the really hard stuff," she says with conviction. "Get through it and learn from it. If you can't deal with it, you are never going to make it."

Zoe's Quest to Help Find Life

In addition to being documentarian on the project, Zoe is studying the weathering process of rocks on Mars. Rocks, it turns out, give up their stories pretty easily. Without even being threatened by a chisel, they tell everything about their history, and on Mars, the rovers have discovered that some of that history has involved water.

"We've found several features in the rocks; coatings, where the outside is a different composition from the inside; cracks with material inside different from the rock—stuff deposited by water. We know water laid down the sediment. But this is water that came through long after that. This shows there have been several episodes on Mars with liquid water," Zoe explains.

The mechanical geologists have not discovered Martian canals, but they have, for the first time, found compelling evidence that Mars once had liquid water on its surface, and in some places, rather abundant amounts of liquid salt water, probably for more than one period. Although the chances are small, it's not inconceivable that a rover could find a fossil embedded in a rock, which would be the first proof of extraterrestrial life.

"I would love to find evidence of past life on Mars," says Zoe. "Going into this mission, I had great confidence that Mars had once been wet. We needed to find the proof. Life is a very important question, but the rovers weren't designed to look for life. They were designed to look for evidence of [liquid] water. If we would find a fossil with the microscopic imager, that would be a windfall and stroke of luck. Future missions will be designed to look for chemical signatures of past life—especially since we've been able to show there was lots of water."

Beside being a boon to the science fiction industry, finding traces of even primitive and ancient life on Mars would be an enormous help to earthlings trying to understand the beginnings of life at home. Earth's active geological history has destroyed any rocks that might have preserved the remnants of tiny, primitive organisms here, and our earliest evidence shows creatures already fairly advanced evolutionarily. With such significant consequences in play, it's easy to see why Zoe is enthralled with her work.

Asking the Most of Her Opportunities

Incredibly, though, Zoe did not immediately jump at the chance to work on the rover project. At twenty-four, she was in her sixth year of a combined math and astrophysics program at the University of Oklahoma, and was already accepted into Harvard's Ph.D. program. One day she came home to an answering machine message from Dr. Steve Squyres, of Cornell University's astronomy department. He was the last person to respond to the round of Ph.D. applications she had submitted to a number of prestigious American graduate schools.

Because graduate applications are sent to departments, not to individuals within the department, Zoe did not know Dr. Squyres or his impressive reputation as an astronomer. Her mind was fixed on Harvard's Ph.D. program, but she called the professor back nevertheless. Over the phone, he described an attractive program at Cornell, and though it sounded excellent, she remained set on Harvard. Perhaps because she knew that even top-notch schools compete for talented graduate students, and because she needed summer employment, she had the inspiration to asked Dr. Squyres what kind of research would be available for her to work on that summer and down the road with Cornell.

"Well, we're sending a couple of rovers to Mars," replied the professor.

"My jaw nearly hit the ground," says Zoe. "'Yeah, you could start working on that if it's something you're interested in,' Dr. Squyres told me."

That tantalizing offer, which came just for the asking, triggered a period of agonizing indecision. Zoe visited her first choice, Harvard, and then Cornell, but in the end, the chance to do something she had thought would be possible only after obtaining a Ph.D. swayed her to Cornell.

The Work Begins

True to his word, Dr. Squyres got his gifted and eager new graduate student involved in the Mars project immediately. Twice that summer Zoe went out to the Jet Propulsion Lab in Pasadena, California, the leading institution for robotic exploration of the solar system and a partner with Cornell. During her first trip she participated in a week-long meeting to welcome new scientists to the team and discuss the scientific goals of the mission. On her second visit she took part in a field test in which a rover model was taken into the desert. The team had to do field geology through the robot to simulate the limitations that they would encounter when operating the rovers on Mars.

In September, Zoe moved to Ithaca, New York, to attend classes at Cornell. For the next year and a half she stayed focused on her courses and continued her study of astronomy. When the rovers were ready to land on Mars, she was able to fly back to Pasadena for eight very special months of work.

The first rover, Spirit, landed on January 4, 2004 Greenwich Mean Time (GMT). Here is Zoe's account of what it was like working at mission control in those days:

> *Early on in the mission, having a shift on the rover was a huge thing lasting ten to fourteen hours. You were going nonstop through it because the rovers were fresh and had all this energy. And you didn't know what you were doing, because this had never been done before. Everyone was trying to figure out how you run a rover twenty-four hours a day. You couldn't work for more*

than four days in a row because it was so taxing. And you [were required] to have at least two days off after that. It did rule your life and we were working on Mars time. The Martian day is thirty-nine minutes longer than an earth day, which means your shift would start thirty-nine minutes later than the day before. You'd start out working in the day, then it would slowly slide, and in a couple of weeks you'd be working night shift. We had to learn to ignore everything that was going on outside. There were no windows opened on the floors we worked on; it was completely blacked out. Our apartment windows were blacked out so we could sleep. It was a very strange experience getting your body to ignore the sun.

Keeping Her Cool

One day near the start of the program, exhilaration gave way to stress. "I was there for what we call 'the Spirit anomaly,' explains the young scientist with professional understatement.

"I was so excited," Zoe says, "because the day before we had planned to use the rock abrasion tool for the first time and I had been part of doing that plan. I went up to the first person I found and asked how the grind went. They had this worried look on their face and didn't really pay attention and said, 'No, it didn't execute and we don't know why.'"

It wasn't until Zoe talked to someone else that she learned about the bigger problem. On January 21, 2004 (GMT), Spirit stopped responding and communicating. During those long, worried sols (Martian days), Zoe recalls, "Those weren't very exciting reports I was writing. My reports had boiled down to a single paragraph about what we had tried and had not worked that day."

Given the time and effort that had gone into designing and building the rovers, you might think that the anxiety about losing contact with the first one to land would have been palpable. But, Zoe explains, "It was not as tense as you would have thought. There was an overwhelming feeling that we'd fix it. We still were hearing a beep. We knew it was alive. A lot of this was helped by the engineers, who never exuded a feeling of defeat. I don't remember ever having a feeling that we had lost it."

And they hadn't. The engineers traced the cause to a software problem. By the time Opportunity landed on January 25 (GMT), both rovers had new software.

Having to Go Home

The mission went relatively smoothly after that. The team even found a way to get off Mars time. "We shifted things so we didn't have to work earlier than six A.M. or later than ten P.M. What ruled our time then was the time we had to talk to the rover, only one chance each day, and the time once a day that data came down from the rover," Zoe explains. "After a while we got more comfortable with what we were doing and our shifts got moved down to about eight hours. Then, after eight months, everything went remote. We all went home." Saying goodbye to such an inspiring group of teammates must have been a little sad, but the compensation for those leaving was getting to work from their own home or office. Working a shift became nothing like it was at first.

The team now uses video or teleconferencing for their meetings. Zoe takes notes and files reports in the comfort of her office at Cornell or at home. Shifts last about eight hours, and the team no longer has to cover twenty-four hours a day, because the mission objectives have been achieved.

The two rovers, on opposite sides of Mars, are still going strong after more than a year, taking pictures, maneuvering toward interesting geological formations, drilling into rocks, taking spectrometer readings, and doing microscopic close-ups. The original mission requirements called for the rovers to last just ninety days. Everything since has been a welcomed bonus.

When Will Her Work Be Done?

No matter how longs these engineering marvels keep going, their lonely, strenuous work has already yielded exciting discoveries, discoveries that Zoe and others will work for years to interpret. As planned, these dutiful six-wheeled explorers are on a suicide mission with no escape. They will die on that desolate planet. The only uncertainty is how long it will take the Martian dust to do them in. Because windshield wipers and aerosol spray cans would have been impractical additions to the weight-challenged design, the rovers' solar panels were built larger than necessary to compensate for some dust accumulation. Ultimately though, fine Martian dirt will settle thickly enough on the rovers' solar panels to slowly starve them of energy. When that happens, the need for documentarians will be over, but Zoe's work as an astronomer will have only just begun.

Outreach, the Last Step in Research

Zoe is not sure where she'll end up once her Ph.D. is completed, but she wants to continue working in planetary studies and exploration with NASA. She also wants to stay involved in education and public outreach, activities she's been pursuing for a few years with Passport to Knowledge, an innovative science program for middle school students. "We talk to a video, very matter of fact," she explains, "giving the audience the inside view of what it's like to be a scientist on this project. We've done six cities and are still going. It's an amazing experience, and the best part is at the end, when the kids can come up to talk one on one. They look at me like I would have looked at someone when I was a kid. I can see that look in their eyes. I just love it."

She's also one of the young scientists involved with Marsapalooza, a rock concert-style tour designed to teach youth about Mars exploration. (See the next section for a website on the tour.)

To Zoe's way of thinking, working with kids completes the research process. "Taking data, analyzing it, coming to conclusions, writing the paper for peer review, and publishing are all steps along the way, but there's one more. You are funded by taxpayers: you should take that knowledge and get it out to everybody so they can understand and enjoy it."

Hardships Make the Victory Dearer

As remarkable as Zoe's career has been, she's had her challenges. Being the only girl in some of her college classes was, from her point of view, anything but an advantage. "The guys look at you as though you're weird. They don't know how to handle you. It's strange."

She persevered in spite of those uncomfortable feelings, and has felt the awkwardness with her male peers finally come to an end in graduate school. "People in the past called you nerds and geeks, but now you are all in a group. I've found the ones who mattered are able to admire you and even think it is attractive that you are so smart. There are those guys out there; you just have to find them." Fortunately, she has.

More challenging, though, has been her mother's health. Zoe's parents were divorced before she was born. Her mother, who is now retired, brought her up on a modest teacher's salary. Her health began to fail when Zoe was still an undergraduate, and a year before Zoe's graduation Ms. Learner was diagnosed with lupus, a serious disease that often has many of the symptoms of arthritis. Then, just weeks before Zoe and her mother were to move from Oklahoma to Ithaca, New York, Ms. Learner suffered a serious car accident that left her permanently disabled.

Zoe cares deeply for her mother and regrets her ill health; she does not resent the time and attention her mother requires. In her characteristically positive way, Zoe says, "I think of it as a way of keeping me honest. So much great stuff has happened. If everything had been easy, my success wouldn't have been such a meaningful experience." When you look at it like that, setbacks make achieving the goal all the more personally significant.

Knowledge + Determination = Money

Like many high school students, Zoe was surprised to learn that Ivy League schools don't give out many academic scholarships. Even as a National Merit Scholar, Zoe was being offered academic loans while her friends were scooping up sports scholarships.

"I had *no* money," she says. The University of Oklahoma was the only school to offer her a full scholarship, including room and board, for five years. "I was so grateful to them," she adds.

On its website, the University of Oklahoma boasts of

having the highest per capita number of freshman National Merit Scholars "among comprehensive public universities" and being in the "top ten of all public and private institutions in the number of freshman National Merit Scholars enrolled." That's no accident. The university offers full scholarships to any National Merit Scholar in the country.

Respect for the University of Oklahoma vies with gratitude in Zoe's heart. "After a very short time there I realized it was an amazing school. I think it was one of the best schools I could have gone to. I don't think I would have done as well if I had gone straight to an Ivy League," she says, with no false modesty. "I would have been completely overwhelmed." Her double degree required six years of undergraduate education; the sixth year was funded by awards and other financial assistance she received from the University of Oklahoma's math and astronomy departments. During her summer vacations, Zoe worked in paid research positions or internships, which she found through her professors or through postings on the bulletin boards of department offices. One of those internships, at the Harvard-Smithsonian Center for Astrophysics, sparked her love of Harvard University and introduced her to scientific conferences.

Now, as a graduate student at Cornell, her tuition is waived and she receives a stipend of around $23,000 per year from the school's astronomy department. In retrospect she sees that even when she was an undergraduate, money was not the problem she thought it was. Most colleges can find a way to help highly talented students if the student is determined enough to seek out every option. As a graduate student, Zoe isn't making a rich living yet, but professors earn very comfortable salaries—not to mention the respect of countless students.

"Do What You Love"

Zoe says the most obvious way to get involved in space exploration is through science and engineering. She counsels students to take more math and science than their school requires, every single year, in fact. Students with a strong math and science background have a wealth of majors to choose from in college. "Feel around to find something that really interests you," Zoe urges. "Do what you love, and then find a way to make it useful to space exploration."

For those who would rather be the plummeting projectile than the person calculating the time of its impact, Zoe says, "That's OK. We can use just about any expertise. We need people to write, artists to draw, people in media, camerapeople, truck drivers, security guards. There's a way for anything to be useful. Follow your passion."

This is good advice in any field of endeavor, not just space exploration. Zoe followed her passion with a determined focus, and it led to Mars. With her combination of qualities and skills, even the sky is no longer the limit.

ON BECOMING A WORLD-CONQUERING SCIENTIST

For any career that requires an advanced academic degree, whether in science or the arts, your most valuable resource is the school guidance counselor. He or she can help you find out more about your area of interest, what colleges are strong in that field and what these schools require for admission and awards. Get to know your guidance counselor at the beginning of your first year in high school so you have time to take the courses required for acceptance to your college program of choice. If you don't quite know what you want to do, don't wait for something to inspire you. Talk to the counselor anyway so you don't miss out on opportunities simply because you skipped one math course or didn't elect to take a foreign language.

Outside of school, seek out people who are doing what you think you'd like to do. Colleges list their professors' areas of expertise with e-mail addresses, which makes it easy to send a perfect stranger a friendly question. Ask a professor how she would recommend you go about arranging to study in her field. From my experience as a journalist, you will not always get an answer but you may hear from someone who really has something to say on the issue. And of course, read as many books as you can about people who are doing what you want to do. Librarians are good at finding books that you might never imagine exist; give them some clues about your interests and watch the hardcovers fly.

ROVING AROUND OUTER SPACE

If you find Zoe's world of space exploration intriging, you can read the full, fascinating story of the Mars rovers by the people closest to it. See "Mission Fantastic to Mars" at marsrovers.nasa.gov/spotlight/20040810.html. The Athena Science Payload site at athena.cornell.edu, describes the instruments on the rovers.

The following institutions have excellent sties on space exploration and general astronomy: NASA (www.nasa.gov); the Jet Propulsion Laboratory (www.jpl.nasa.gov); the Harvard-Smithsonian Center for Astrophysics (cfa-www.harvard.edu); and Cornell University, Department of Astronomy (www.astro.cornell.edu).

ZOE'S BOOK RECOMMENDATIONS

Zoe selected three titles from among her favorites: *Contact* and *Pale Blue Dot*, both by Carl Sagan, published by Simon and Schuster, 1985, and Random House, 1994, respectively; and *The Smithsonian Book on Mars*, by Joseph Boyce, published by the Smithsonian Institution Press in 2002.

ZOE'S TOP PLACES TO VISIT

If you're thinking of doing some space exploration here on Earth, try one of these fascinating destinations: Meteor Crater in Arizona; the Lowell Observatory in Flagstaff, Arizona; the Jet Propulsion Lab in Pasadena, California; the Kennedy Space Center in Cape Canaveral, Florida; or the Johnson Space Center in Houston, Texas.

MORE ABOUT OUTREACH PROGRAMS

Zoe is primarily involved with the following outreach programs, which seek to educate their audiences on matters that touch her both professionally and personally: Marsapalooza (www.nasa.gov/audience/foreducators/5-8/features/F_Marsapalooza.html), funded by the National Science Foundation (NSF) with support from NASA; Passport to Knowledge (passporttoknowledge.com), also supported by NSF and NASA (the unit "To Mars with MER" is loaded with mesmerizing info on the rovers' accomplishments); and the Lupus Foundation of America (www.lupus.org).

WORRIED ABOUT ACADEMIA FOREVER?

You may hear people suggest in a vague, hushed sort of way that academic careers are sought by perpetual-student types who are too timid to get a job in the real world. In fact, academic positions for graduate students and professors are highly competitive and require planning, determination, and talent just like most anything else worthwhile. As Zoe's career demonstrates, academics do not sequester themselves in an ivory tower but make important contributions to the world by exploring it (sciences) or interpreting it (the arts). Academics don't always lead a monkish life of teaching and study, either. Many Ph.D.s work in industry or business as well, often commanding big bucks.

Of Mentors & Manatees

ANDY GARRETT

MARINE SCIENTIST & MERMAID RESCUER

To anyone who loves being outdoors—particularly on the water—and working hands-on with unusual wildlife, Andy Garrett's job will seem ideal. Andy is a marine scientist who rescues sick and injured manatees. He works at one of five manatee field stations run by the Florida Fish and Wildlife Conservation Commission. Besides overseeing all the captures and rescues of manatees in the state of Florida, Andy conducts research to advance our knowledge of these endangered, gentle sea mammals.

Manatees, AKA sea cows, are placid, slow-moving animals that were sometimes mistaken for alluring mermaids by mariners of yore who were, perhaps, on the verge of sunstroke. A manatee up close is no pinup girl, and despite having nothing of beauty for which to be hunted, manatees are struggling to survive. They are frequently killed in collisions with motorboats, subject to entanglement in nets, ropes, and debris in waterways, and sensitive to stress in cold weather. Many manatees are killed by red tide, a naturally occurring eruption of algae that release a neurotoxin which paralyzes manatees and causes them to drown.

Although it's impossible to know exactly how many manatees call Florida home, the Fish and Wildlife Research Institute, a division of the Florida Fish and Wildlife Conservation Commission, conducts an aerial count of manatees at the coldest time of the winter, when they frequently sunbathe at the water's surface to keep warm. One recent tally put their number at just over 3,200.

If manatees were mermaids, each and every one would have a giant crush on Andy Garrett. Just a day before our interview he rescued a desperately ill mother and her calf near Naples, Florida. The pair was taken to a zoo in Tampa for care. Only the week before, Andy's team rescued another ailing mother and calf at the same location. The team transported them to SeaWorld, where the mother, who had kidney disease and problems with her lungs and digestive system, subsequently died; her calf is thriving.

"Both these mothers were so sick, yet they were still nursing their calves," says Andy. "It's amazing that they were still being mothers in a deteriorating situation."

The Making of a Manatee Superhero

The twenty-eight-year-old scientist says his love of the water and the creatures in it began when he was a child. Every summer for more than fifty years his family locked the door of their Wheaton, Illinois, home and headed off to a cottage on a Missouri lake. Andy spent many blissful weeks of his childhood swimming, water-skiing, and catch-and-release fishing. "I was always fascinated to think there was life under the water. I used to put breadcrumbs on the water and watch the fish feed," he says. He even remembers his first trip to the ocean when he was ten: "I'd never seen a jellyfish before. I ran up to it and picked it up by its back while my parents were screaming for me to put it down." He didn't get hurt, and he didn't lose his curiosity about things aquatic.

A presentation at his high school by a representative from Eckerd College introduced Andy, then a junior, to

Eckerd's marine biology program. The next year during spring break he visited the campus in St. Petersburg, Florida, with his parents, and "fell in love with it." He later signed on for marine science with a concentration in marine biology.

A Volunteer Job Leads to a Paying Job

Andy had to find paying work during his summers and Christmas vacations in high school and college, but he squeezed in time during the fall of his senior year in college to volunteer at the Florida Marine Research Institute. He worked with the fisheries group scanning otoliths, or fish ear bones. Fish and manatee ear bones have growth rings, just like the rings of a tree. "Slice it, put it on a slide, stain it, and count the rings," he says, describing his routine there. It may not sound like much, but that volunteer commitment said a lot about Andy's dedication to the field.

At this time, too, Andy was taking a marine mammals class from the famous Dr. John Reynolds, a world expert on marine mammals and chairman of the federal Marine Mammal Commission. Dr. Reynolds told Andy about a volunteer position opening up at the lab with which he was associated, near Eckerd College. There, Andy helped with the salvages and necropsies of dead manatees. "I started volunteering at the lab in the spring," recalls Andy, "and within a month of graduation I had a job."

Andy believes his volunteer time at this lab is what put him in line for his job, so it's no surprise that he's a strong advocate of volunteering. "Volunteer as much as you can to get your foot in the door," he says, though he cautions that the job has to excite you. "It opens up other doors you wouldn't even think of."

The Importance of Mentoring

In addition to being his professor, Dr. Reynolds was an important mentor to Andy. Unlike many mentoring situations however, their relationship did not start by chance. Eckerd College assigns each student to a professor who then oversees the student's undergraduate program. Andy took the initiative to ask Dr. Reynolds to become his official mentor. "The system basically forces you to hook up with a professor who can help you," says Andy, who seems thankful he was required to take what can seem like a giant leap to make personal contact with a professor.

At work, Andy has been lucky to have the help of

another very influential mentor, Dr. Sentiel Rommel, a good friend of Dr. Reynolds, as it happens. "Dr. Rommel is said to be the number one marine anatomist in the world," says Andy. "He's been a mentor to many of us, and just getting involved with him gives you so many more options because he knows many people. Someone like that can give you advice on where to go and what not to do and what worked for him when he was up and coming."

"The cliché goes, it's not what you know but who you know. I don't totally believe that, but I do believe it's important to associate with people who can help you out, to speak to people who work in the field you're interested in, because they know of avenues you have no idea about, and they have friends who may be able to help.

"Dr. Rommel will tell you he had a lot of people looking out for him when he was coming up, so he feels that he owes it to the rest of us. To me, an important part of mentoring is remembering that people have helped you and then in turn doing something for other people."

In his turn, Andy encourages his current volunteers. Asked if people of modest strength can work in the field with marine mammals, he says with the wisdom that's characteristic of a good mentor, "There are roles for everyone, of every size. There are lots of women in our groups. You're not limited by your size."

There's Danger, Too

Andy's job does require a lot of physical strength to deal with the dangers that capturing thousand-pound manatees can pose. One particularly challenging capture brought those dangers home.

"The animal started spinning in the net," Andy recounts. "Once that starts, the net turns into a big ball of twine. The net started wrapping around my hand like a medieval torture device. It just kept turning. Everyone on the boat heard pops, and I thought my wrist had been broken and my elbow was next." Somehow he got his hand free. His wrist was grotesquely swollen, his fingers white and boney. Tendon and ligament damage remain, though nothing was broken.

"I'm six-foot-four, 225 pounds. If it had been someone else it probably would have been a lot more serious. Everyone who gets on that boat knows the risks."

Those who do get on that boat experience the reward of helping these unusual creatures, and they've decided that learning more about them is worth the risk to their personal safety. The risk to the manatee, though, is a little harder to judge. "You have to weigh the benefits versus the risks of catching the animal," says Andy. "Do I risk this animal's life stressing it out, when it is already debilitated, to bring it to a rehab center where it will be treated for its injuries and probably get better?"

Once rescued, the manatee is brought on board a boat that is low to the water and then quickly brought to shore, to be carefully placed in a truck and whisked to an oceanarium at a zoo or an aquarium for treatment and rehabilitation.

When treated animals are released, the young ones and those that have had to stay a long time in the rehabilitation center are tracked by satellite. Andy's team attaches a belt with a small torpedo-like tracking device around the manatee. At two months, six months, and one year they locate the manatee to check its health.

"From everything we can see, the tracking device doesn't bother them at all," says Andy. "We've had people extensively watch these animals and they'll reproduce, they'll give birth, they'll do everything with these tags on. The belts have safety breaks on them so if the animals do get entangled, the belts will break off." Once the team is convinced the animal is thriving, they recover the tracking device and wave a fond goodbye.

With healthy animals, captures are less ethically fraught. As long as an animal can be captured without being injured, there's much to be learned. Andy and his wet-suit-wearing team conduct a rigorous physical on each captured manatee for research purposes. They check its temperature and heart rate. They hoist it up with an overhead winch and weigh it. They collect blood samples to check for infections and major organ functioning. They measure the thickness of the fat on its back as a general indication of health. They take urine to determine if it is normal, and fecal samples to figure out what the animal has been eating. They also collect microswabs from the animal's nose, eyes, and other orifices to check for funguses, bacteria, and viruses. If they have captured a lactating mother, they take milk samples as well. With these necessary indignities quickly over, the manatee is tagged with a microchip like the ones available for house pets. Then the team snaps a picture of the manatee and releases it. The microchip allows the team to identify the animal should they encounter it again, and the picture is compared to other pictures to see if this manatee has been seen before.

And Sadness...

Unfortunately, much of Andy's work with the research institute involves dead animals. His tone changes when his conversation turns to dealing with them, and it is clear his encounters with so many of them saddens him. Until he was given a promotion and put in charge of the Jacksonville field station, Andy was on a team of six at the Marine Mammal Pathobiology Lab in St. Petersburg where necropsies (autopsies) are performed on manatees to determine why they died and to learn more about their biology and habits in order to better protect them. All manatee carcasses in Florida are sent to this lab, which also collects and stores frozen kidney and blubber tissue samples for future study.

Mechanical Aptitude Comes in Handy

Transporting these cow-sized bodies to the lab is no trivial task. Manatees average about a thousand pounds and round out at about ten feet long. Very mature ones can weigh more than a ton and be longer than twelve feet. The usual flatbed trailers rot from the water of the melting ice used to preserve these massive bodies and the trailer end gates have been known to slip open, depositing hazardous manatee carcasses on Florida highways. Andy designed a trailer that holds a U-shaped bed made of thick cutting-board plastic bolted onto frame that is welded to the trailer. The carcass is winched up into the bed, the back of the trailer is barred with a gate, and the animal is covered with ice and canvas. This trailer won't rot or corrode and holds the animals much more securely.

Andy's ingenuity has led to numerous design modifications copied in many manatee rescue boats. Before Andy arrived on the scene, manatees were being hauled out of the water into skiffs designed for Florida's mullet fishery and not much changed from the 1900s. Andy added a fly bridge, which is a driving platform that is elevated above the deck; the added height expands the field of vision as the boat moves through the water. He had bilge pumps installed to bail out the water that's taken on board during a capture, as well as installing the overhead winch for weighing the animals.

Andy is always looking for ways to make rescues and transport easier and more efficient, and being able to design some solutions himself has already allowed Andy to make a notable contribution to his field.

Travel as a Perk

Andy travels throughout the state of Florida to assist other field stations and agencies with their manatee captures. He's also been sent to Belize and Puerto Rico to help with their manatee programs. In the summer of 2003, he was asked to help with a different kind of marine animal: California sea lion pups were dying off on account of a naturally occurring biotoxin, demoic acid, that affects the adults. Andy and a coworker were sent to the California Marine Mammal Research Center in Sausalito to help.

"Adults were abandoning their pups, and the pups were washing up on shore. In the morning they'd have nine or ten pups that needed to be necropsied. A lot of them had abscesses on them, which we didn't understand, but they also had ulcers in their stomachs and other problems often seen in animals abandoned by their mothers.

"There were almost a hundred animals in cages," Andy recalls. "We'd help feed them and restrain them while they were getting their shots." He also got to see the release of some elephant seal pups that had come to the rehabilitation center before the sea lion crisis. "With the release of a single manatee there are so many people and lots of logistics, but they just loaded these pups into a cage on the back of a truck and drove to a remote beach, put a ramp up, and watched them all slide out into the water. That was a lot of fun." Fun and meaningful.

The Reward

Saving the life of an animal, especially an endangered one, is hugely rewarding. Knowing that your research is furthering the chance of survival for a whole species must be equally gratifying.

Andy has done a lot of good for the world, and so have his mentors. With their help, a dedicated and enthusiastic young man with a unique skill set has been able to make a rich contribution to marine mammal biology. By fostering Andy and others like him, these mentors are enriching their field and have the satisfaction of seeing their own work furthered through the vision and achievements of a new generation. That's a big payoff, which is why even the most accomplished of people, like Dr. Reynolds, choose to be mentors for young people with talent, drive, and the courage to approach them. Andy says he can't thank his mentors enough. One day there will be those who feel the same way about him.

MARINE SCIENCES: SIGN ABOARD!

"So You Want to Be a Marine Biologist: The Revenge!" was written by someone who seems to have done it the hard way. This funny and irreverent piece addresses high school students' practical questions about what courses to take in high school, what college attend, and how to get into graduate school. You'll find the article on Milton Love's wild and wacky site, which he calls "The Love Lab" (www.id.ucsb.edu/lovelab/revenge.html).

Milton is a marine biologist of considerable standing, judging from his resume and the treasure chests of grant money he's hauled in, but read his site and see if you don't think the guy is a cross between Hemingway and Monty Python.

To see profiles of marine scientists working in Florida and advice for those wanting to do the same, visit the Florida Fish and Wildlife Research Institute site, (research.myfwc.com/education/interviews/interviews.asp). Andy's profile is there, too.

CAREERS IN MARINE BIOLOGY & OCEANOGRAPHY

The Hopkins Marine Station of Stanford University website (www-marine.stanford.edu/HMSweb/careers.html) offers an extensive list of resources about jobs and careers in marine biology and oceanography, including marine mammal science and training.

VOLUNTEERING IN WILDLIFE MANAGEMENT

Volunteer opportunities in wildlife and habitat management are available for people of all ages. Andy uses volunteers throughout Florida to check on manatees that are reported sick or injured. Volunteers work in labs and sometimes even help with rescues. Check out the websites of your state wildlife conservation commission and of environmental groups in your area for opportunities with animals and habitats near you.

Florida's Fish and Wildlife Conservation Commission, for example, works with sea turtles, fish, coral and other invertebrates, sea grass, and many more animal and plant species. To learn about the commission's internship and volunteer program, which features opportunities throughout the state, check out its website (research.myfwc.com/features/category_sub.asp?id=2139).

MORE ABOUT MANATEES

Do you want to know how old manatees get, or where they live and why they are endangered? You'll find an extensive bibliography, with a special section for young folks, at (www.seaworld.org/infobooks/Manatee/home.html).

Florida's Fish and Wildlife Research Institute has lots of information online about manatees and about the institute's research projects and rescue efforts (research.myfwc.com/features/default.asp?id=1001). You can also see Andy in a photo of the pathobiology lab.

ANDY'S BOOK RECOMMENDATIONS:

Three of Andy's favourites are *Introducing the Manatee,* by Warren Zeiller, published by University Press in Florida in 1992; *Manatees: Our Vanishing Mermaids,* by M. Timothy O'Keefe, revised edition published by Larsen's Outdoor Publishing in 1995; and *Manatees and Dugongs,* by John Reynolds and Dan Odell, published by Facts on Files in 1991.

HELP PRESERVE MANATEES

The Save the Manatee Club protects manatees in Florida and around the world. You can "adopt" a manatee through this organization (www.savethemanatee.org). Its offices are located at 500 North Maitland Avenue in Maitland, FL 32751; you can reach a staff member by phone at 407-539-0990 or toll-free at 1-800-432-JOIN (5646).

The Wildlife Foundation of Florida helps fund manatee research. Donations can be earmarked for manatees at (wildlifefoundationofflorida.com).

For those who live in Florida, purchasing a manatee license plate is a great way to support manatee research and rescue, and a primary source of its funding. Check it out at (research.myfwc.com/features/view_article.asp?id=7613).

WANT TO TRAIN DOLPHINS?

Dolphins and whales are the Marilyn Monroes of the marine mammal world. Placid manatees don't have much interest in show-stopping antics, but other marine mammals get plenty of spotlight, which means there is somebody who gets paid to play with Flipper all day. The site www.dolphintrainer.com, written by marine animal professionals, provides information and extensive resources on marine mammal care and training. It offers links to professional organizations, such as the International Marine Mammal Trainers Association (IMATA); universities and colleges that have marine mammal programs; public facilities that display marine mammals; government agencies; and research and stranded animal rehabilitation centers. Among the books the site recommends is its own, *Starting Your Career as a Marine Mammal Trainer.* You'll find an order form on the website, or you can send an e-mail with questions or comments to DolphinTrainer01@aol.com. For more information, contact DolphinTrainer.com, 1370 Trancas Street #402, Napa, CA 94558.

Working Hard, Working Smart

STEVE BURSKY

MUSIC INDUSTRY TALENT MANAGER

In a business where first contacts are usually made by phone, Steve Bursky has something of an advantage. "They don't know I'm a college student right off the bat," he says. "I'll have deep conversations with people about the industry over the phone or be talking about a deal and then when we meet in person, they're looking over my shoulder for Steve."

Steve's youthful accomplishments in the music industry have provided him with a level of access that many others dream about. In the summer of 2003, after his third year of college, he found himself in the office of arguably the most powerful recording industry executive in North America, the president of Sony Records in New York City. "That was a thrill. If I'd been thirty instead of twenty-one, I can't imagine he'd have been as receptive to me coming in and taking so much of his time," says Steve. "I've tried to meet as many important people in the industry as I can while I'm still somewhat youthful and unintimidating," he adds, "because as soon as I'm doing this full-time, I'm just another guy out there trying to make a living."

That's Steve all over—modest but shrewd, and earnestly hardworking. With one more year to complete a degree in communications at the University of Pennsylvania, Steve is already managing three musical acts, including the hot indie band Dispatch, the group that got him started in the music management business right out of high school. Although Steve plays piano and trumpet and has always had a love of music, his entry into the music management business was something of a fluke—but a reproducible one.

Doing Good Was the Start

"I was very involved in philanthropic work in high school," says Steve. He spent one summer building houses on Tortola in the British Virgin Islands, and in the beginning of his senior year of high school he and a couple of other students started a food bank in Fairfield County, an area that includes his hometown of Greenwich, Connecticut.

Meanwhile, a graduate of Steve's posh private academy, the Brunswick School, was the bassist for a band that was developing a buzz on the prep school and college circuit. Known at the time as One Fell Swoop, and later renamed Dispatch, the band gave a concert at Brunswick School early in Steve's senior year. The success of that event prompted Steve to ask the band to do a benefit concert in May. The county's fledgling food bank received $40,000 from that performance.

The impressive organization that Steve marshaled to bag that much money led the band's manager, Greg Brown, to offer him a job as assistant manager to the band. He accepted the offer. Steve's first responsibility was to help develop a rep program that would give fans incentives to promote the band. Fans could, for example, buy ten CDs for sixty dollars and sell them for ten dollars each to make a profit, or, in exchange for guest passes to concerts, they could put up posters in music stores and distribute flyers to advertise a new release or an upcoming concert.

"Dispatch started as a New England band focused on building Boston and New York and playing to a lot of northeastern colleges," says Steve, "and now they are a national band playing to people across the country in every market." The group has put out four studio albums, one live album, and one DVD. Steve credits Napster and file sharing as the major way Dispatch's music became known. "Dispatch was a pioneer in this alternative way to build a band," Steve says. "They were able to build a following from scratch without a major marketing mechanism, a label, behind them."

Right Time, Place, Person

Steve's responsibilities with the band continued to increase through his freshman year. This put him in a good position to take over its management in 2002 when Greg, the full-time manager, left.

Since then, Steve has added two other clients to his roster, Rich Price, and The Ally, and his contacts have spread across the United States. "Management is a very exciting part of the industry because you have your feet in every part of the business," he notes. "A typical day can include talking with your booking agent to schedule tours and decide who is going to play on the bill with your band, working with promoters in different cities to arrange ticket on-sale dates and what newspapers you want to advertise in, then maybe talking to your lawyer in New York, who's working on a publishing agreement, then to a publisher out in LA who's putting together another opportunity."

Steve gained the sophistication to juggle all these things from working with Greg Brown, and acquired the connections from his association with a sought-after musical property. "If I hadn't had the opportunity to work with Dispatch, there's no way I'd be where I am right now, because they were and continue to be such a hot band. There are so many people courting them, from booking agents to publishers, that I was able to use these contacts for additional projects," Steve explains.

"I reached out to the band and they made me an offer after that, but I was in the right place at the right time," says Steve. "I feel very lucky that I was the one who caught their eye at the time they were needing somebody to help out."

On His Own Terms

Steve is modest about his good fortune, but he is selective about the people he associates with. "This industry has the reputation of being slimy and drug-infested," he says pointedly, "but it doesn't have to be that way if you value the right things, surround yourself with the right people, and make the right decisions. I parted ways with a client because our values were different," he says, speaking of a musician who signed with a major label almost immediately after they went their separate ways. Steve knew he would lose out on some significant money by releasing this artist, but his position is unequivocal: "If I can't relate to someone's values, I can't work with them.

"I have been lucky," Steve continues, "to surround myself with people in the industry I respect." His modesty may be endearing, but his determination to put values first keeps his playing field pretty clean.

Not surprisingly, his parents have had some reservations about his line of work. "When my mother heard I was working for a rock band, the first thing she said to me was, 'Do they do drugs? I don't really want you to do this.'" But, once Steve's parents met the Dispatch members, their fears evaporated. "They're three of the most clean-cut, straight-edge guys," declares Steve. "They never picked up drugs in their lives, barely even drink. After shows, they just go to sleep." It took that meeting, says Steve, for his parents to trust his judgment.

That judgment may be put to the test when Steve graduates and tries to land a job with a big music management company in New York, Boston, or Los Angeles. He'll bring his acts with him, which will mean change for him and them. A large firm has abundant resources—interns, experienced workers, powerful contacts, industry-leading deals. For Steve, the challenges may include a loss of autonomy and because he would no longer have final say, there could be a shift in his relationship with the artists under his management.

Continuing to Do Good

In the meantime, Steve continues to organize an annual charity concert at the University of Pennsylvania. He says the college administration believes it is the largest student-led fundraiser on any American campus. One concert raised nearly $50,000 for the Cystic Fibrosis Foundation.

Steve is also branching out into executive producing. He is currently helping an artist put together a CD by connecting him with producers, helping him negotiate pricing, and assisting him with other aspects of making a new recording.

As for the money, Steve says his first job in the industry

paid more than anything else he could have done, and he hasn't looked back. "In management, if you get one act that breaks, you can live nicely," he says. Most managers, Steve reports, earn 15 to 20 percent of what their acts earn before expenses. Steve's breadwinning act is Dispatch, though the band members have been taking a break to pursue solo opportunities for some months now.

Like most hard-driving entrepreneurs, Steve feels his life lacks balance. "I'm always working," he says. "I'm thirsty to get things done and have an endless drive to help these bands get to the top."

For those who think the long hours are worth the gratification of seeing talent get opportunity and recognition, Steve recommends getting involved with the rep program of small bands as a start. "Don't be shy. Reach out. Unfortunately, a lot of this industry is about who you know," he says. "If you can open the door with someone, you're in good shape. The ones who are persistent without being annoying, who have the passion and drive and do the hard work, are the ones who end up making it." They're also the ones who, like Steve, feel a rush of excitement like none other when the talent they've discovered gets a break because of their efforts and their smarts.

One Year Later

When he graduated from college in May, Steve didn't sign on with a big management company. Instead, he opened spacious offices of his own by the Hudson River in New York City. He's also got a recording label of his own, Foundations Records, an imprint of Universal Records. "A lot of things have happened," he says with characteristic modesty.

By staying in touch with his industry contacts, he made it known that at graduation he was looking to join a large talent management agency. He also maintained regular contact with record industry executives to keep them up to date on his musicians' achievements. That's how, three months before his graduation, Steve came to invite the executive vice president of Universal Records to see one of his clients, Stephen Kellogg & the Sixers, in concert. This executive VP, as it happens, is the brother of the president of Universal Records. "They were impressed with the alternative, grassroots approach that we had, the following and community building," says Steve. The Universal executives saw an opportunity to align with a young, talented manager with promising artists, and Steve saw a chance to build his own company with the financial support of an industry giant.

Steve opened his New York office one month after finishing college. The mission of Foundations Records, like Foundations' management, is to build long-term careers through a bottom-up, grassroots approach. Steve now has his own interns and is actively signing on more artists. Ownership of his company is shared with Steve's long-time mentor in the business, Dalton Sim, and a friend of Dalton's who has extensive experience in starting up record labels. They have one full-time staff member. Universal Records covers much of the company's overhead, including a good chunk of the office rent. Universal also finances all of Steve's record deals and distributes all the company's records, but Steve has claim to his artists and controls all the marketing. When the initial term of his contract with Universal has ended, he can renegotiate it or walk away. "Our goal is to build a name for ourselves so in a few years we have people knocking on our door hoping to be the next one to negotiate with us." Right now Steve seems to have the best of all worlds: artistic independence backed by the deep pockets and full distribution capabilities of a major record company.

Besides wishing he had more staff in the office, Steve's biggest problem these days is coping with the extensive traveling he must do to organize and attend showcases and tour launches for his growing roster of artists. He's busy and he'll get busier, because his roster needs to keep growing. It's been a year since The Ally broke up, and Dispatch is no longer playing together. Before Dispatch dispatched themselves, they recorded a live CD and DVD of their July 2004 concert in Boston, which Steve says was the largest independent musical event in U.S. history, attracting 110,000 fans. The story of that concert and the way Dispatch changed the independent music business is now a movie, titled *Last Dispatch*.

Given his fast and furious rise, was school more an impediment than a help? "My education has definitely helped," he says. "If nothing else, it gave me analytical thinking skills, a sense of how to speak to people, how to write and communicate—all things we look for when interviewing interns."

Through all this, Steve has remained a remarkably grounded guy who stays in close touch with his family and worries about his work/life balance. Looking ahead to an almost unprecedented vacation—ten days in Spain with his parents and sister—he said, "Hopefully I'll be able to stay away from the cell phone."

Steve has accomplished a lot in a short time. The temptation is to think of him as some kind of business genius, a guy who was born with an uncanny savvy about how the world works, but in fact he's just good at finding out how to get things done and getting skilled people to help him. He uses his youth to his advantage and makes the most of his contacts. Although he is diligent, driven, and tireless, he is not overcome by ambition. He's been able to nurture his business on his own terms and associate with people he respects. That, perhaps more than anything else, reveals the intelligence of this hardworking manager.

To gain entry into the music business, consider joining a rep program. Band managers organize these programs as a way of encouraging fans to promote the band. Steve Bursky suggests e-mailing a contact on a band's website and asking what you can do to help. "You'll be surprised how many responses you'll get," he says. The manager himself is likely to reply if the band is small. Show your enthusiasm by pitching in when asked, and you could very well learn firsthand what other fans only get to read about in magazines.

The Pollstar site (www. pollstar.com) lets you search by city, band, or venue to see where groups are playing and what live music is coming to your town. "Go see shows and find out what you like," Steve advises. "Introduce yourself. Go to small venues and see the bands rise up the ranks and build an audience." It's nice to be able to say you were there from the beginning, but it's even better to be able to say you helped make it happen. "Be the one to bring them to a record label," exhorts Steve. "To me it's about being proactive and not waiting for someone else to discover the talent."

INTERNSHIPS

For an insider's view of the industry, nothing beats working as an intern at a major label. "Most music internships are unpaid because there are so many kids who want them and so few spots," says Steve. Again, who you know helps a lot in securing one of these enticing positions. Steve has obtained internships for some of his school chums, so build your contacts, beginning with rep programs, and move up.

One outstanding site, Starpolish, posts requests for internships and jobs as well as openings for these positions; go to www.starpolish.com, "Velvet Rope," then, "Labor of Love." Starpolish offers lots of seasoned information on getting a band off the ground, launching a solo career, and managing and producing. Click on "Advice" and "Resources," and check out the postings on Velvet Rope.

MUSIC MANAGEMENT COURSES

Colleges and universities that have music programs may

also offer a music management degree at the undergraduate or graduate level. These programs combine music education with business training. As Steve Bursky's story shows, however, a degree in music management is not always a prerequisite for success. Business savvy, people and communication skills, a passion for music, and a discerning ear are the bedrock qualifications.

Two schools with respected music business programs are New York University (education.nyu.edu/music/mbusiness/u1.html) and Berklee School of Music (www.berklee.edu/departments/mbm.html).

CHARITY WORK

Would you like to organize a benefit concert at your school? Perhaps a grad is making some waves in the music world. Graduates are the easiest to approach because they may have some lingering affection for the old alma mater. Without that bit of luck you will have to find a band that is small enough to agree to do a high school benefit but big enough to draw a sizable crowd. Once a band has pledged to play, though, your job should become easier: large charities employ knowledgeable people who may be willing to help you organize an event as long as it's big enough to justify their time. If you're unable to find a charity to help, you have a great excuse to reach out to band managers and ask if they have been involved in benefit concerts. If the answer is yes, ask for contact information for the organizers of the charitable events. With one call you will have made two connections, and the ball will be rolling in this who-knows-who business.

Many colleges have student-run concert committees that bring live music to campus. Volunteering for the concert committee will give you a taste of the live music side of the industry and an appreciation of what goes into organizing a large public event.

GRAB ON TO NEW TECHNOLOGY

"Digital music is our future, and amazing things are popping up through the development of technologies like satellite radio," says Steve, who urges those coming up to stay on the cutting edge of technology and watch for trends. Check out XM Satellite Radio (www.xmradio.com) for a taste of the combined power of music and technology. By the way, XM Satellite Radio plays unsigned, independent, and emerging artists, and they're looking for reps...

STEVE'S BOOK RECOMMENDATION

Steve recommends the fourth edition of *All You Need to Know About the Music Business: Revised and Updated for the 21st Century*. Written by Donald S. Passman and published by Simon and Schuster in 2003, it is widely considered the most comprehensive guide to the music business. Steve's entertainment lawyer suggested he read an earlier edition when he was negotiating his first contract for Rich Price. Enough said.

One Step Along the Trail

ANNIE SOCCI

OUTDOOR EDUCATOR

"My brother said to me once, 'You're really good at getting paid for things you like to do.' I *have* gone out of my way to find jobs that are a little unusual," says Annie Socci, and she's not afraid to move on from a job that she's not passionate about.

Annie, twenty-five, is an outdoor educator for Outward Bound USA, a nonprofit organization that provides teens and adults with adventure-based education programs world-wide. In the fall, Annie puts together dog sled teams. In the winter she takes groups into the wilderness with dog sleds and cross-country skis. Summer finds her canoeing in the Minnesota boreal forest with at-risk teens.

"I really believe in the ability of the wilderness to tell you who you are," she says. "By being able to teach them the skills they need to survive, I'm making a positive impact on people's lives."

The Minnesota base camp of Outward Bound USA is tucked away thirty miles from the Ontario border in eastern Minnesota. It is one of four Outward Bound wilderness schools in the United States and one of the groups that offer the Intercept program, a wilderness adventure course for teens and young adults who are "struggling" but not yet in "serious trouble."

Wilderness Adventure with a Purpose

Annie tells numerous stories of teens whose poor choices and adversarial relationships with their parents have been turned around by the Intercept program. Depending on the nature of the outdoor adventure, Intercept programs run from twenty-two to twenty-eight days. Parents are required to attend a three-day seminar at the end of each program. "We teach tools for conflict resolution and anger management. We teach parents and students how to use these tools to create a common language. We try to provide a forum for the family to have an honest conversation that might not have been possible at home. Ideally they can take that process home with them." The successes, she says, "keep me from feeling like I'm just goofing around here."

Even if she were just goofing around, it's not hard to see why her job has kept her away from graduate school for three years. Annie works primarily as a field instructor. She takes groups of no more than seven students into the woods for four to twenty-eight days with only one other instructor. The shorter-range goal is to teach wilderness skills, but the underlying goal is to expand the participant's estimation of their own capabilities. "We'll take people with no wilderness experience whatsoever, and a couple dog teams and a lot of skis and winter equipment and head out for an expedition," says Annie. "We teach them to ski and mush and travel miles a day. As instructors we back off so, ideally, by the end of a course they should be traveling almost independently, depending on their age—mushing their own dog team, navigating by themselves."

Taking the Good with the Bad

Before the winter begins, Annie is in charge of training and conditioning the school's fifty-five dogs. Most of these dogs are Huskies, some of them descendents of the Mawson

Huskies donated to the program in 1992 after an international agreement that banned all non-native species except humans from Antarctica. (The Mawson Australian research station in Antarctica still used dogs at that time.)

Every fall the Outward Bound school hires two or three people to train the dogs, build their endurance and strength, and configure the teams to reduce the potential for fighting among the dogs. Fifty-five dogs have to be turned into eight-dog teams.

Of course, the job is not just mushing into the midnight sun. Annie scoops a lot of poop, too. She does sled repairs and gets equipment ready for the season, in addition to teaching the interns the ropes and training the instructors to run the dogs. Sled dogs, Annie notes, normally have one musher their whole life. Their dogs have to take commands from the trainers, the instructors, and then the students—all in the course of a few months.

While the Intercept program lasts only a few weeks, other students may stay for a semester. These students spend a week at base camp building the sled they will depend on during their subsequent three-week wilderness expedition. A group of seven students and two instructors will have two sleds and two dog teams. But there's no joyriding for students. They ski in front of the sled, making tracks for the dogs to follow, while the mushers run behind, jumping on occasionally.

"I've seen moose and deer and loons and bald eagles," notes Annie. "Sometimes our huskies howl and the wolves howl back. Last summer a bear dragged a food pack away from our camp while we were hanging the packs up in a tree. I followed the bear's tracks while clapping so I wouldn't surprise him. When I saw the bear I let him keep the pack and ran back to camp. In the morning I recovered what was left."

Because Annie is a contract employee, she is hired by the season, as opportunities permit. She regularly has April and September off, though she often takes advantage of instructor training courses in April, such as one that involved mushing nearly two hundred miles from Gillam to Churchill, Manitoba, the northern town famous for its polar bears. Instructors have to pay for these trips, but the training sustains their excitement and their skills.

Seeking Opportunities

Annie has always shown a lot of initiative in seeking out career-advancing programs. Between her junior and senior years of high school in Queens, New York, she took part in a two-month environmental sciences internship program at Cornell University. There she received her first instruction in independent research and put it to immediate use. Birds were eating into local farmers' revenues by scooping their blueberries. Annie found that simply by spraying sugar water on the ripening berries, she had an ecologically friendly solution. The birds got stomachaches when they ate the sprayed berries, but it didn't harm them or the berries. Annie says the professor who was supervising her project published a paper about the finding with Annie listed as lead researcher. "It was great to apply to college with a publication credit," she says modestly.

The next two summers Annie worked as a camp counselor, and from her sophomore to her senior year in college, she was paid to instruct fellow Cornell students in paddling, winter camping, rock climbing, and other outdoor activities that they enrolled in for physical education credits. All this experience is useful to her now in assisting troubled teenagers and young adults.

In the summer after her sophomore year, Annie landed a position with the Cornell Biological Field Station Summer Internship Program. At the Oneida Lake station in upstate New York, she helped collect long-term data on trout and perch feeding patterns and wrote a paper on her findings. This entry-level position became the important foundation for far more adventurous assignments.

A Courageous Request Becomes a Turning Point

Annie recalls the fateful day during her junior year in college when she walked into the office of her favorite professor and said, "You do field research in Costa Rica every year and you have a house down there. Is there any way I could do independent research in Costa Rica for my honors thesis?" To her relief and amazement, the professor agreed. He had never taken an undergraduate student to Costa Rica with him before.

"I always look back on that one thing," Annie says. "I was afraid for months, but finally I walked into my prof's office and said, 'Is there any way?' I feel proud I had the courage to ask, even if later I've asked for other things and gotten a no." Annie spent six months in Costa Rica on a leave of absence from Cornell to do her honors thesis on lizard egg-laying behavior, and learned Spanish while she was there.

Immediately after her college graduation, Annie applied for a three-month biology intern summer program through the University of Arizona. The position involved research in Tanzania, a country on the east coast of central Africa. "When I applied for that job they said, 'Wow, you worked in Costa Rica for six months. You've got international research experience.' That was a huge in." She spent three months in Africa at Lake Tanganyika, one of the oldest bodies of fresh water in the world, sampling and surveying snails and crabs to explore their co-evolutionary relationship. Her research, added to the investigations of others, helped to show that in this lake, over the course of evolution, snails grew harder shells and crabs grew stronger claws.

Annie returned from Africa to a plum teaching position at a swank private boarding school in rural New Jersey. The school was run by the mother of one of Annie's friends; the sixth grade science teacher had quit suddenly. "I literally accepted the job just days before getting on the plane to Africa," Annie says. "I hadn't planned on it, but it seemed like such a great opportunity, and I needed a job. They said, 'You've done field research in three countries; you must really have a passion for science.' So I feel strongly that any little thing like internships that you do really opens the door and makes people take a second look at you." Annie jokes that people probably want to find out whether she was "brave or dumb" to take on some of these challenges. But anyone who meets Annie knows that, while she may be brave, she isn't dumb.

A Summer Job That Became Much More

Although she enjoyed teaching immensely, Annie wanted to go on to graduate school to continue her studies in conservation biology. A friend of hers suggested she become a summer paddling instructor for Outward Bound. She applied, intending it to be just an adventurous summer job before starting graduate school.

"Being in the wilderness is a challenge for me," Annie says. "I was reminiscing about all the experiences I had had in college when I was taking other college students out in the wilderness, and how satisfying that felt. I wanted to experience that again.

"When I got to Outward Bound, I found I really liked the community, the challenge of the job, and the organization. When I learned they had a winter program, I applied for it, and that's where I've been ever since." A big part of Annie's attraction to Outward Bound is the Intercept program and its philosophy of taking responsibility for your choices and for who you become.

A Career of Great Jobs

Annie's job is an enviable blend of outdoor excitement, humbling physical challenges, and inspiring human contact. As much as she loves it, she is giving herself only one more year with Outward Bound. She has the discipline to quit a job many would hold on to with a white-knuckled grip. Annie has left a great teaching position before. She possesses a confidence in herself and an optimism about her next job that let her move on without hesitation.

Biology, Annie believes, will give her even more satisfaction and enough outdoor adventure to keep her excited. So graduate school still calls. "Conservation biology is my main goal," she says. "I have always imagined becoming a professor, doing field research, teaching." A series of terrific jobs has positioned her well for a future in biology. She's acquired the outdoor survival skills to do fieldwork just about anywhere in the world and the teaching experience to be at least an above-average lecturer. It's possible Annie will later find other jobs that take her outside academia because so much of Annie's attitude and initiative seems to be leading to a fabulous career of many great jobs.

EDUCATION WITHOUT DOORS

Outdoor/wilderness education is often known as experiential education; Internet searches on any of these three descriptors plus the word "education" turns up interesting programs around the world. To begin exploring outdoor education programs, as a participant or as a teacher, check out dmoz.org/Recreation/Outdoors/Schools_and_Education and www.outdoored.com. To learn more about Outward Bound, go to www.outwardbound.org. In addition to instructors like Annie, Outward Bound hires a small number of seasonal interns in exchange for room and board and a modest stipend.

The National Outdoor Leadership School, at nols.edu, is another well-known wilderness skills and leadership training organization with many locations.

OTHER OUTDOOR PROGRAMS FOR TEENS WITH DIFFICULTIES

Second Nature Wilderness Program, at www.snwp.com,

offers wilderness therapy in Utah and Georgia for troubled teens.

SOAR (Success Oriented Achievement Realized) specializes in adventure camps for LD, ADHD, and ADD preteens, teens, and adults. Check it out at www.soarnc.org.

JOBS IN THE GREAT OUTDOORS

Your own Internet search for outdoor jobs is bound to yield many choices. A good place to start is www.wilderdom.com/joblistings.html. For jobs in Canada, try www.paddlingcanada.com/jobs.

SCIENCE INTERNSHIPS FOR HIGH SCHOOL STUDENTS

Contact the colleges, universities, and museums near you to find out what they offer. Cornell no longer offers the summer research program that Annie attended, but other institutions offer similar internships. Boston University offers a program for minority high school students at www.forsyth.org/forsyth.asp?pg=100068.

Princeton accepts a few interns in a program that addresses topics not generally covered by orthodox science, such as psychic research and precognition; you can learn more at www.scientificexploration.org/yi/internships.php.

Most paid internships are intended for college students but with some luck, a seriously ambitious high school student may be taken on as a volunteer. Hundreds of biology-related internships for college undergraduates are listed at career.ucsb.edu/students/majors/biology.

Don't forget to talk to your science teachers about summer opportunities and about science competitions like the Siemens Westinghouse Competition in Math, Science & Technology, at www.siemens-foundation.org/competition.

The Courage to Change the World

JASON WEST

MAYOR AND SOCIAL ACTIVIST

When you're convinced that even members of Congress are "just people," it's not that hard to run for state legislature at the age of twenty-three. Jason West took a run at state office twice. On his first try, he had a budget of $500, donated by family and friends. He doubled this less than princely sum two years later and won about 2.5 percent of the vote in the New York State Assembly election. He is known to say he lost both elections by a landslide, but he got enough attention to raise some issues as part of the debate. Three short years later, at the age of twenty-six, Jason became mayor of New Paltz, a pretty town of six thousand in upstate New York. His campaign budget—enough to buy a beater of a car if he wanted one—was $2,600.

Politics Started Out Personal

Jason's political awakening began when he was an undergraduate studying fine arts and history at the New Paltz campus of the University of New York (SUNY), where he helped organize a student protest against the governor's plan to raise SUNY tuition fees and decrease student aid. Three hundred people turned up outside a bookstore where Governor George Pataki was signing books. "[We were] chanting, handing out leaflets, making speeches on a blow horn about the governor's policies," says Jason. "He came out and I saw the fear in his eyes. That's when I realized that these political figures aren't monumental, powerful creatures that can't be touched. They're just regular people with powerful connections."

After that protest, Jason joined the Green Party in New Paltz and became active in helping its candidates get on the ballot and in organizing other protests. Soon his political education took a different turn. He was arrested, along with about six hundred others, during a sit-down demonstration in an intersection near a meeting of the

International Monetary Fund and the World Bank, and found himself in a grim District of Columbia jail overnight.

"Eventually," Jason says, "my friends and I were tired of telling people what we didn't want. We decided to come up with positive solutions and run for office so we could put them into practice."

Not Being Intimidated by Power

Jason is an ardent advocate for the ordinary Joe, and he doesn't suffer from hero worship. "Never let someone in public office make you think they're smarter than you or have any more common sense than you," he says passionately. "I've met dozens of state legislators and members of Congress and they are no different from anybody else; they're no smarter, no better organized, have no more common sense." There is no disrespect, exaggeration, or arrogance underlying this statement. Jason fervently believes that ordinary people have the skills to participate in government and that they must participate to ensure the health of democracy and to provide lawmakers with the enlightened leadership that will create broad social equality.

Jason does concede that most elected officials have two

advantages that most ordinary citizens don't—more personal wealth to help pay for election expenses, and the support of a party's leadership. But that shouldn't discourage would-be office seekers, he says. Election money and party support can be gained by a candidate doing it right.

Jason rallied the Green Party behind him for his mayoral bid. He did this, in part, by showing his commitment to environmental issues in his town. In the time leading up to this race, Jason became a volunteer member of New Paltz's environmental commission and eventually became the committee's chairperson. Then, in 2003 a Green Party slate of three, which included Jason, was elected to the town council of the Village of New Paltz, and formed the majority. With that election victory, Jason became one of five Green Party members in elected office in New York State and one of more than two hundred Greens elected nationwide. The defeated incumbent mayor was a seventy-two-year-old doctor who had been New Paltz's mayor for sixteen years and deputy mayor for four years before that.

Driven by Conviction

In his first term in office, Jason has overseen the construction of one of three planned artificial wetlands to deal with the village's sewage sludge. The liquid sludge is spread over a bed of reeds that break down the organic waste without odor or artificial chemicals, an innovative approach that Jason says is being used around the world.

Jason also gained national visibility by presiding over the weddings of twenty-five gay couples. "When I ran for state legislature, someone from the audience at a candidates' forum asked everyone their stand on gay marriage," he recalls. "I said then that I was in favor of full marriage equality. Because mayors can perform marriages in New York State, I realized I had the power to right a wrong and that I had a moral obligation to do it." He has since been served with an injunction prohibiting him from solemnizing more gay marriages. He also had twenty-four criminal charges laid against him for performing the marriages while knowing that the couples lacked a marriage license. With the help of a lawyer who offered his services pro bono, Jason challenged the charges in court. Ultimately they were dropped, but if he had been convicted, he could have gone to jail for a year and been fined a thousand dollars for each charge. Despite these possible consequences, Jason is convinced he did the right thing and that the law is lagging social enlightenment.

In addition to his marriage equality advocacy, the young mayor is also working to establish affordable housing, environmentally friendly public transportation, and the use of solar energy at town hall. These initiatives are all in keeping with the Green Party platform of social justice, grassroots democracy, environmental responsibility, and nonviolence. It's a platform that seems to hold appeal for the town's youthful community. Three quarters of the town's residents are under thirty-five years old, and the average yearly income is a modest $24,000. Many of the residents are students at the New Paltz campus of the State University of New York (SUNY).

New Paltz has a municipal budget of $4.5 million, thirty employees, and is responsible for water, sewer, roads, schools, and development through zoning laws. When Jason took office in the spring of 2003, the job paid $8,000 a year. To supplement this salary, he kept up the jobs he'd had since leaving college: running his own house-painting business part-time and performing with Arm-of-the-Sea Theater—a troupe, its website says, that explores "contemporary themes through the ancient traditions of mask and puppet theater." The theater company travels to schools, cultural centers, and festivals in a bus that burns a vegetable-oil-based fuel.

At the beginning of Jason's second year as mayor, the town council voted him a $10,000 raise, so he is no longer painting houses or performing stories with puppets. Now he supplements his salary with speaking engagements around the country, in which he shares his views on marriage equality and the importance of participating in the political process.

Passionate Advocate, Reluctant Speaker

Jason is often asked to speak about politics and grassroots democracy to youthful audiences. He's frank about the challenge of changing entrenched power relationships in politics. "Kids who are cynical are absolutely right," he says. "That doesn't mean you shouldn't do something about it." If you work smart, you can punch considerably above your weight. Jason advocates working at the party level to influence the candidate selection right off the bat and, as he has done, getting involved in small communities "where money doesn't matter in the election, so anybody can run." Swing ridings—voting districts that can go either way—are often hotly contested, but offer great opportunity for the committed to be heard and to influence the vote.

Asked how he got to be so self-confident, the young

mayor quickly shoots back, "I'm not. It's all a front." It's hard to believe this good-looking guy who radiates confidence is putting it on, but he says public speaking did not come easily to him.

"I hated speaking in public, but my friends brought me to poetry readings, where I read some of their poetry and my own awful stuff, and I got comfortable with a small audience that way," he says, "When you're speaking about something you believe in, it gives you a lot of confidence. All you need is conviction, common sense, and an ability to listen to people," he adds. And courage. "By having the courage, I mean being nauseatingly nervous when you get up to speak—your palms are sweaty and you can't sleep the night before—but doing it anyway even though you're exhausted and nervous and scared, because it is the right thing to do."

Jason believes that people respond to personal conviction. "People will respect you for taking a stand one way or another even if they don't agree with you."

That respect is something every person in public office is working for, and a young politician's family might be hardest to get it from. Jason's father has a housepainting business and his mother is a secretary. No one in his family is political, and for a long time they thought and probably wished he'd grow out of it. Once he actually ran for office, Jason says, he received instant attention from the media and a greater measure of respect from his family.

Anyone Can Do It . . . and Should

"Activism isn't a phase," Jason says with conviction. "It's a lifelong commitment. I spoke to Pete Seeger yesterday. He's in his eighties and he's been an activist since his teens." Jason intends to run for a second term as mayor. Beyond that, he will admit to no plans—not even law school. "Not being a lawyer is not a handicap at all, because there are lots of lawyers around. We have an attorney on staff. If you are going to have government by the people, you can't be restricted to certain occupations and income levels, which is what happens all too often in politics."

Clearly not one to be intimidated by title, money, or influence, Jason wants to see more people become politically active because he is profoundly confident in the ordinary citizen's judgment and good sense, especially because most citizens are outside the established spheres of influence. That's why, he says, anybody can do the job, and why he's so committed to getting young people to become politically engaged.

Public office will not make you rich, but it offers rewards of a different kind. "When you change the world," says Jason, "it is the most exciting and fulfilling thing you can do, and it is possible: you just have to have the courage to do it."

Jason developed his courage by becoming engaged in political issues that immediately affected him. He saw firsthand that people in power are like most other people, except that they have money and friends with influence. He became convinced that personal conviction can build grassroots democracy. But he also worked strategically. After two tries at state office, he set a more modest goal. He directed his energy to a small town where he thought he could make a difference and where he could win. And win he did. Though Jason doesn't know where his quest for social justice and environmental responsibility will take him, he hopes that along the way he will inspire more of us to take an active interest in the political process so that together we can change the world.

CHANGING THE WORLD 101

For most of us, a job in politics combines the worst of all worlds—job insecurity, stress, lack of privacy, and low public esteem. But as Jason has demonstrated, politics can be rewarding, meaningful, and done with integrity. Public service is a calling that deserves more respect than it gets, and becoming involved is a good antidote to the twin pitfalls of helplessness and cynicism. The best way to get a grip on issues, and the public institutions that grapple with them, is to start at the local level in your community.

VOLUNTEER

Every town and city has a council that directs various committees, which in turn are always looking for volunteers. Jason, you'll recall, was a volunteer on the New Paltz environmental commission. He suggests sending a letter to your town council explaining that you'd like to volunteer. If the council recommends a committee, follow up by contacting the chair of the committee and asking what kind of help they need. If you don't receive a reply, don't take it personally. Follow up with another letter, or call the council directly. Age shouldn't be an issue as long as you're reliable. If you do volunteer, you'll get a running view of an area of concern in your community, along with the chance to meet some local politicians.

In the United States, municipal politics and national parties are aligned. (In some countries, such as Canada, local politicians are not associated with a national party.) Besides asking for money, party websites describe the party platform and explain how you can participate. Most political parties have a youth wing that can be accessed through the main site.

VOLUNTEERING WITH U.S. POLITICAL PARTIES

What follows, in alphabetical order, are the most prominent U.S. political parties, along with their websites: the Democratic Party, www.democrats.org; the Green Party, www.gp.org; the Libertarians, www.lp.org; the Reform Party, www.reformparty.org; and the Republicans, www.gop.org.

Volunteering for a party or candidate during an election

campaign is a surefire way to see democracy in action. People are always needed to distribute pamphlets, make signs, and do a hundred other behind-the-scenes jobs. Your help will be most appreciated and, with luck, you could be rubbing elbows with some political junkies whose wisecracks alone are a crash course in politics.

If you are truly ambitious, you may want to get involved at the state or federal level. The government hires students in their junior year of high school as pages in state legislatures and in the U.S. Congress and Senate, and many other opportunities abound.

Explore the many options in volume 5 of *Community Service for Teens,* titled *Participating in Government and Politics.* The author is Bernard Ryan, Jr., and the series is published by Ferguson (Factsonfile.com).

READ

Newspapers can seem flat and dull until something you have an interest in is reported; then they're better than a slug of Mountain Dew. Pick one issue and follow its coverage. Or work the other way around: try to get coverage for something you're committed to and watch the press at work—a guaranteed education.

DEVELOP

Leadership and public speaking abilities are important for anyone with ambitions in areas that require strong social skills, like politics and business. Consider programs that foster leadership and community involvement, such as Boy Scouts of America (www.scouting.org) and Girl Scouts of America (www.girlscouts.org), cadet programs like the U.S. Naval Sea Cadet Corps (www.seacadets.org) and community service clubs with a youth wing, like Rotary International. Participating in a high school debating club is a quick and cheap way to gain experience in public speaking, and you'll find out pretty fast if you are good at thinking on your feet or need more practice. (Knowing the subject area is a big confidence booster.)

Jason's leadership skills, he says, came from taking the initiative to get things done. He stresses that what you need is "the confidence to make decisions and accept that you are going to make mistakes and not be paralyzed by that."

A BURNING IDEA FOR A COMMUNITY PROJECT? DON'T LET A LACK OF MONEY STOP YOU

There are abundant resources available to young people who want to take part in community service initiatives.

Two not-for-profit organizations with a mission to provide know-how and funding for such initiatives are Youth Service America (www.ysa.org) and Youth Venture (www.youthventure.org).

Companies and service organizations can also be a source of funding for well-conceived projects by young social activists. The most generous of these is the BRICK Awards, which give a $5,000 scholarship and a $5,000 grant to each winner eighteen years old or under, and $10,000 grants to winners between nineteen and twenty-five. This award honors and funds young people who have helped fix a problem in their community. It has been described as the Oscar of youth service awards and is sponsored by Do Something (www.dosomething.org), which also sponsors the $500 Do Something Grant (see below).

Other company-sponsored recognition awards include the following:

1. The Very Best in Youth Award, sponsored by Nestlé USA, makes a $1,000 donation to a nonprofit organization selected by the winner. To be eligible a student must be between nine and eighteen and must demonstrate a "tangible" contribution to school, church, or

community, in addition to good citizenship and strong academic achievement (www.nestle-verybest inyouth.com/vbiny/home.jspa).

2. Build-A-Bear-Workshop® "Huggable Heroes" Contest recognizes people eighteen years old or younger who have "demonstrated extraordinary service in time, effort and results for causes that make a difference in the quality of life in their local community." Prizes include a donation to a cause chosen by the winner (www.buildabear.com/aboutUs/community/hug gableheroes/default.aspx).
3. Kohls Kids Who Care gives scholarships to six- through eighteen-year-olds who have demonstrated outstanding compassion for others (www.kohlscorporation.com/CommunityRelations/Community05.htm).
4. Prudential Spirit of Community recognizes middle and high school students who have done exemplary volunteer work. State winners receive a $1,000 award and national winners receive $5,000 each. Two winners from each state are selected each year (www.prudential.com and search on "Spirit of Community.")
5. Angel Soft Angels in Action awards people eighteen

or younger for community involvement. Eighteen winners are selected (www.angelsoft.com/angelsin action/awardsprogram.asp).

6. The National Caring Institute gives out six awards annually to young adults who "ennoble the human race by transcending self in service to others" (www.caringinstitute.org/caringawards.html).

With thanks to Becca Robison, www.astrotots.org

Established awards are great, but the competition for them is usually intense. Don't overlook companies in your own neighborhood that may be happy to support a worthwhile initiative and get the favorable publicity that goes with it. When you find a business that seems like a good fit with your project, ask for help. You may be delighted by the generosity of community-minded people who own small businesses.

DO SOMETHING: THE MAGAZINE

Do Something is dedicated to helping young people who want to change the world through activity in their own community. Free to many high schools, it's produced by Do Something, a national not-for-profit organization "whose mission is to give young people the tools, inspiration and opportunity to make a difference." The website continues: "We want young people to get off their sofas and into their communities to *do something* about the problems they see." Do Something sponsors innovative programs and makes generous awards for exemplary community youth projects (www.dosomething.org).

READ ABOUT THE POLITICAL SYSTEM

The League of Pissed Off Voters (www.indyvoter.org) aims to engage turned-off and cynical students and young adults "in the democratic process to build a progressive governing majority in our lifetime." The website goes on to describe the group's achievements and strategies. Under "Resources and Links," it provides extensive information on electoral politics and candidates, election reform and voters rights, money and politics, voter registration, voter organizing projects, student organizing, alternate media, articles, activist tips, and so on. The site leans heavily to the progressive side but there are enough listings to keep even a conservative surfing for hours.

Making the world a better place, as we all know, requires

something that no amount of resources, money or reading can provide. These help, of course, but world-changing action requires unusual insight into a problem and the creativity of a workable solution—things that do not stand on education, social position, or physical attributes, so here's to all who dare to put their conviction on the line to change the world.

Epilogue

DIFFERENT STORIES, SHARED INSIGHTS

I feel privileged to have been able to take a snapshot of the lives of these dynamic people and their exciting careers. But I confess that when I set out to seek people under twenty-seven with dream jobs, I carried with me certain assumptions about the people I would likely find. I assumed they'd all be bright, I expected them to be privileged, and I imagined they'd be full of themselves. Wrong on two out of three counts. They are bright, but most of the people who are featured in these pages are not from privileged backgrounds, and despite their inspiring accomplishments at an impressive age, they're almost universally humble about themselves and their achievements. Perhaps in an unspoken way, they're aware that success is not achieved in isolation—it depends on many other people whose support brings about the breaks. Even the most introverted and independent of our bunch, Mike and Jerry of *Penny Arcade*, owe their ability to make a living off their comics and writing to a businessman who believed in them and put his livelihood on the line by agreeing to work for them.

NEVER STOPPING

Another personal quality our ten heroes share in abundance is drive. In the face of setbacks and disappointments, they kept going. Zoe cares for an ailing mother while pursuing some of the hardest academic disciplines known to man. Mike and Jerry, were eating a much too steady diet of Chinese noodles, and Mike shared lodgings with rats. Jason, the mayor of New Paltz, New York, lost two elections in a row. Ryan, sports manager and fundraiser extraordinaire, was abruptly fired from a dream job. Freddy keeps getting shut out of the press gallery for the Academy Awards. (OK, that's not so bad, but the insult stings anyway.) Insulated by their vision and drive, these people roll with the punches. "Who said it was going to be easy?" could be their collective motto.

With this drive comes a certain impatience, a dissatisfaction with things as they are, an eagerness to get to the next level. Steve works tirelessly to promote his musicians. Annie doesn't want to stay in any one job, no matter how wonderful, for too long. Amy wants to place more service dogs with young children and heighten awareness of the benefits of this pairing.

MISTAKES GO WITH THE TERRITORY

Everyone profiled in this book has stretched emotionally and financially to move forward. With these efforts go risks and, inevitably, mistakes. Perhaps the most valuable thing I've learned from these fascinating people is their attitude toward mistakes: they are simply the inescapable cost of learning. Those who are mortified by mistakes and minor failures cannot go forward. Just keep moving ahead. Freddy said it eloquently when he repeated the advice he'd received from Will Smith: "Never let your success go to your head and never let your failures go to your heart."

YOU CAN'T GET WHAT YOU DON'T ASK FOR

This internal fortitude shows itself another way, too. Not one of the people whose stories are told within these pages is afraid to ask for what they want. They don't always find it easy, like Sabrina who still secretly cringes when someone new looks over her portfolio. But they all ask. Repeatedly. As a habit. They make sure other people know what they're out to accomplish and what help they are looking for. Sabrina wants to show her work to high profile photographers so they'll hire her on future assignments. She calls them up cold to ask to visit them. Freddy wants interviews with hot celebrities. He asks them in person. Annie wanted to do research in Costa Rica. She asked her professor if she could camp at his summer house. Zoe wanted interesting summer work and asked a prestigious professor whom she'd never met what kind of work he could offer her. Some of these requests took awesome guts, but like making mistakes, it's all part of doing the hard stuff. The distance between assertiveness and pushiness is much wider than most of us think.

WHO YOU KNOW DOES COUNT

One more telling thread in these stories is the usefulness of contacts. Ryan has gotten his jobs through contacts he diligently put together and maintains in the sports industry. Steve's own record label came from being able to invite the

Vice President of Sony Records to a concert. Andy's job at the lab came about because his professor and mentor was a friend of the lab's director. Amy got serious about pet therapy because a friend of her mother's worked at a nursing home. Whether we like it or not, no one gets along on the sheer brilliance of their work. The world is a network of people, people exerting influence where they can, often for the benefit of those they believe in. Keep an organized record of those you've been lucky enough to encounter who might one day be able to help you. Maintain communication with them, and, like Ryan, keep letting them know what you want and where you are going. Everyone loves a winner, and most love the thrill of helping someone become that winner.

Of course, winning means something different to every person, but somewhere in there, among all those different values and dreams, is a shared belief that success is being true to the best part of who you are and making the most of your talents. It's not easy to do this. The world is a competitive place, a Darwinian struggle, but it's not a Mad Max nightmare either. The ten people profiled here have turned their skills and interests into fulfilling and exciting careers. Armed with the knowledge of how they did it, you can do it, too. Dream jobs are there for the taking or the making. Seize the confidence to transform your passion into your future, and one day maybe you'll say, like Mark Twain, that your work has been play.

Acknowledgments

The idea for this book is not my own. Rick Wilks had the brainstorm. Rick was introduced to me by Sheryl Shapiro, whose warmth and encouragement are responsible for this book being in existence.

There were many who suggested interesting people to talk to and many more whose worthy stories did not make it into this slender volume. Thanks to you all for your enthusiasm and understanding.

To those who do find themselves within, thank you, too, for letting me tell your stories and for the generous help you provided along the way, including many useful references.

Eden Edwards and her tireless team at Houghton Mifflin deserve many thanks for giving shape to this book.

And finally, the biggest thank you of all to my family—to Arthur, for his unwavering support in every way; Nathan and Ruth, for their indulgence; and Roslyn, for her help with the manuscript. If it takes a village to raise a child, it certainly takes a family to write a book.

—Donna Hayden Green, November 2005